# THE TALMUD
# FOR BEGINNERS

# THE TALMUD FOR BEGINNERS

## Volume 3

## Living in a Non-Jewish World

### Judith Z. Abrams

A JASON ARONSON BOOK

ROWMAN & LITTLEFIELD PUBLISHERS, INC.
Lanham • Boulder • New York • Toronto • Oxford

A JASON ARONSON BOOK

ROWMAN & LITTLEFIELD PUBLISHERS, INC.

Published in the United States of America
by Rowman & Littlefield Publishers, Inc.
A wholly owned subsidiary of The Rowman & Littlefield Publishing Group, Inc.
4501 Forbes Boulevard, Suite 200, Lanham, Maryland 20706
www.rowmanlittlefield.com

PO Box 317
Oxford
OX2 9RU, UK

British Library Cataloguing in Publication Information Available

**Library of Congress Cataloging-in-Publication Data**

Abrams, Judith Z.
  The Talmud for beginners / Judith Z. Abrams.
    p.  cm.
  Includes bibliographical references and index.
  Contents: v. 1. Prayer.
    1. Talmud—Introductions. 2. Talmud. Berakhot—Commentaries. 3. Prayer—
Judaism. I. Title.
BM503.5.A27  1991
296.1'2061—dc20                                    90-1211

ISBN: 0-7657-9967-7 (alk. paper)

Printed in the United States of America

☉™ The paper used in this publication meets the minimum requirements of American
National Standard for Information Sciences—Permanence of Paper for Printed Library
Materials, ANSI/NISO Z39.48-1992.

For Arthur Kurzweil
He fulfills the teaching,


"Make your study of the Torah a regular habit,
Say little but do much,
Receive everyone cheerfully."

*(Pirkei Avot* 1:15)

# Contents

# Acknowledgments

This volume is the third in a trilogy aimed at introducing learners to the joys of Talmud study. The first *Talmud for Beginners* explored the tractate of the Talmud that deals with prayer. The second sought to take readers to a higher level by examining the role of text study in their lives. In this book, we will look at how to maintain one's Jewish identity in a non-Jewish world. Thus, in this series, we have progressed from the most private way of relating to one's Judaism to an outward orientation.

One way of envisioning spiritual progression is as an ascending spiral. We explore 360 degrees of our environment while continuing to move upward. This means that we encounter the same issues time and again, we just meet them on a higher plane. Thus, the outward trend of this series of books is not meant to be a one-way trajectory, from center to periphery, but rather as a sweep that brings the traveler back to the core of the experience, enriched from an exploration of the boundary between Judaism and paganism.

The process of writing these books has been a spiritual journey for me, personally. In the first book, I found my voice. It was pure joy to transmit my love of Talmud through the written word. The next book was written while I was immersed in the academic atmosphere of Baltimore Hebrew University, working on my Ph.D. The present book brings me full circle, but I hope at a higher level, to my love of the text and the rock-solid belief that it holds the key to a fulfilling, meaningful life through the practice of Judaism. I hope my work is richer for having made this journey.

I am grateful to God for allowing me to make this journey and for giving me the opportunity to publish these works. Arthur Kurzweil has my deepest gratitude for his openness to new ideas, for his willingness to help me in this work, and for his love of Talmud. I am also most grateful to my teachers, Dr. David Kraemer of the Jewish Theological Seminary and Rabbi Joseph Radinsky of United Orthodox Synagogues in Houston, for opening the world of the Talmud to me and for reading my manuscripts.

Several persons helped me in writing this book. Rabbi Shaul R. Feinberg, Associate Dean, Hebrew Union College-Jewish Institute of Religion, Jerusalem, provided me the information on the "House of David" Inscription on a Victory Stele. Rabbi Nathan Laufer of the Wexner Heritage Foundation recommended that I read the book *Idolatry*, which greatly helped me organize my thinking on this topic. Elaine Kellerman, director of the Bureau of Jewish Education in Houston, graciously provided me with the *Highlights of the CJF 1900 National Jewish Population Survey*. Rabbi Joseph Radinsky, Naomi and Bob Hyman, Robert Reichlin, Nada Chandler, Christopher Benton, and Steven Abrams read over the manuscript and made many suggestions that improved it immeasurably. I am grateful to them for their time and effort.

I would also like to thank the students to whom I taught this material. Their insights strengthened this book immeasurably. The original class to whom I taught this material included Esther Abadie, Paula Eisenstein Baker, Paula Bottecelle, Sharon Endelman, Iris Fisherman, Arza Funk, Ann Glazier, Judy Goldman, Sadie Kaiser, Linda Kates, Jeanie Krim, Jeanne Saletan, Shirley R. Schnoll, Debbie Seigel, Eric Simon, and Libby Wolf. The insights of the members of the Houston Jewish Educator's Council class are also evident in this book. The participants in that group include Shirley Barish, Shirley Burkom, Vivian Coggan, Steve Daum, Esther Freedman, Debbie Ostrow, Nancy Picus, Harold Reingold, and Lisa Stone. The class at Congregation Emanu El in Houston, including Christopher Benton, Freddie and Alford Bleeker, Nada Chandler, Alan Jones, Naomi Kertesz, David A. Levy, Steven Lutzker, Stephen Miller, Robert Reichlin, Curtis Tatar, and Elizabeth Weinberg, were a source of inspiration. The members of my Monday night class, John Akerman, Barbara Baruch, Joy Friedman, Evelyn Eyzaguirre, Bernice Kaufman, Rose Rose, Marcia Schneider, Kate Sexton, Sondra Shapiro, Howard Stern, Beverly Sufian, Jeanie and Joe Victor, and Joel Winograd, helped me understand the difference between superstition and faith.

Of course, I am grateful to my husband and greatest helper, Steven, and to our three children, Michael, Ruth, and Hannah, for the love, joy, and meaning they give to my life. They are my greatest teachers.

# Introduction

If you have ever read spy novels, you know that one of the main tasks of an infiltrating secret agent is to thoroughly understand the culture the spy is bent on subverting. The operative learns the language and the culture, makes friends with the natives, and tries to fit in in every way so that he or she can then destroy the enemy. The spy must almost *become* the enemy in order to vanquish his foe.

## Paradigm Shifts

Before we can understand tractate *Avodah Zarah*, which means "Strange Worship," the volume of the Babylonian Talmud that deals with idolatry, we must go through a similar process. We will not be able to understand the sages' violent reactions to idolatry unless we truly understand idolaters' practices. This will be difficult because to really grasp this religious system, we have to step out of two mindsets—our Jewish frame of reference and our modern one—and go back to the world that spawned idolatry. We will only be able to understand the sages' reactions to idolatry if we understand the phenomenon itself.

This changing of perspective has been called a "gestalt switch" (Kuhn 1970, 204) or, more popularly, a paradigm shift. In his classic work, Kuhn describes the way science progresses. One paradigm, or way of looking at the world, works and is fleshed out until it ceases to explain significant problems. Then a competing theory emerges and a conflict between adherents to the old and new schools ensues. Eventually, the new theory triumphs because its adherents outlive its opponents.

The battle between idolatry and monotheism can be seen in this context: idolatry, appealing to statues that embody different forces of the universe, was in competition with monotheism, a devotion to one deity alone who could not be embodied or pictured in any way. When the sages composed the tractate of the Talmud we are going to study, and indeed, when all of biblical literature was created, adherents to these two competing theories warred against each other. Thus, we begin to see what caused the bitter rhetoric against idolaters and idolatry that we will read in this tractate. The polemics in this tractate may well seem overdone to the modern reader. When this seems to be the case, replace the word "idolater" with "Nazi," for example, and the meaning will become clearer. The sages saw idolatry in a way akin to the way we experience Nazism: an ideology that fosters a complete breakdown in faithful human relationships; in short, the enemy. Jews and idolaters believed in competing ideas that each felt best explained the phenomena they observed around them. Each strongly believed they were right and that the other side was wrong.

We in the West no longer believe that praying to statues is an effective means of worship. This makes it difficult for us to understand the depth of this conflict, and hence the rhetoric we will read seems overblown and mean-spirited. After all, monotheism won and idolatry lost. To understand the sages' world and viewpoint fully, we have to take the fervor with which different political approaches to peace are expounded in Israel today, for example, and transfer, in our minds, the vitality and desperate importance of that debate back into the conflict of monotheism against idolatry in the rabbinic era (700–500 c.e.). To truly understand, we will have to be "spies" and attempt to comprehend, as best as we are able, what idolaters saw in idolatry. Then we will have a more honest appreciation of why the sages characterized idolatry as they did.

Investigating the idea of idolatry may bring up uncomfortable issues regarding the difference between faith and superstition. What was sincere faith three generations ago may be this generation's superstition. For example, three generations ago, if you were standing in an article of clothing that was being sewn, you held a piece of string in your mouth in order to stop all your intelligence from being sewn out of you. To the modern ear, this dictum sounds ridiculous. To those raised with it, however, it was an obvious precaution, as logical as wearing one's seatbelt seems to us today. To understand this tractate, we must shift twice. We must abandon our concepts of "magic," "superstition," "faith," and "medicine" and adopt the sages' boundaries for the phenomena denoted by these words. Then we must shift again and see things from an idolater's perspective if we are to be able to step back into a world where idolatry was the overwhelmingly popular religious choice.

Reading selections from this tractate and keeping your balance, so to speak, will take effort. You may be faced with uncomfortable choices you had not considered before now about how to maintain one's Jewishness, how to partake in a non-Jewish society without being engulfed by it, and how important it is to have a clear image of what one wants out of life Jewishly. Some resources have been cited in the Bibliography for those who want to pursue these practical questions in greater depth.

### How Idolaters Saw Idolatry

What is idolatry? It is not, as we commonly believe, the worship of mute, lifeless statues. The statues are merely a focal point for meditation and devotion. According to Thorkild Jacobsen, in his classic examination of Mesopotamian religion, *The Treasures of Darkness*, idolaters related to their gods with three major religious metaphors:

1. As *elan vital*, the spiritual cores in phenomena, indwelling wills and powers for them to be and thrive in their characteristic forms and manners. The phenomena are mostly natural phenomena of primary economic importance.

2. As rulers.

3.  As parents, caring about the individual worshiper and his conduct as parents do about children.

Of these three different ways of viewing and presenting the gods, the first would appear to be the oldest and most original, for it is the one that is never absent. . . . The second metaphor, that of the ruler appears to be later. . . . [Then] the major gods became national gods, identified with narrow national political aspirations. [pp. 20–21]

Jacobsen's summary shows that idolatry itself was a developing, changing entity. Idolaters related to the gods in ways that changed as their societies and sophistication developed.

So, if idolaters were aware that the gods they worshiped were not contained in statues, nor even in the heavenly bodies with which the gods were associated, how did they see their deities in relationship to these physical symbols? There are three possible ways of seeing this relationship:

1.  The god is the star.

2.  The god [can be seen] as an institution and the star as the building in which the institution is housed. The institution's building is often a convenient way of identifying the institution, but obviously the institution's identity will be preserved even if it is moved to another building.

3.  An alternative model for the relation between a god and its associated star is the relation between the mind and the body, where the god is the mind and the star is the body. The god dwells in the star as the mind dwells in the body. . . . When a god is described as being fixed to a star, the fixed relationship is generally a punishment for rebellion, which transforms the god into an entity lacking freedom and limited in realization of its desires. [Halbertal and Margalit 1992, 142–143]

Jews and non-Jews differed in the ways they conceived of this relationship:

We can put it roughly this way: the view that the god of the sun is identical with the sun is the view that the monotheist attributes to the idolater. The view of institutional identity between them is the attribution of the neutral observer. But it is the mind–body relation as the model for relation between the god of the sun and the sun that is apparently closest to the view of the sun worshiper himself. [Halbertal and Margalit 1992, 143–144]

Judaism characterizes idolatry as foolish and unsophisticated, a childish worship of what one sees rather than devotion to the single essence at the heart of all creation that is true faith. However, that is not how idolaters viewed themselves. Idolaters might well witness a Jewish Torah service, in which the Torah is extracted from the ark with great ceremony, crowned and reverently kissed, as a fetishistic, superstitious rite. Jews would know that they were not worshiping the Torah but expressing reverence for its importance in their lives as the expression of God's word. This may provide us with our first inkling as to why the Gemara (see below, "This Tractate's Structure") concentrates so consistently on inner states. Worship depends, in large part, on what is happening *inside* the worshiper. Only the individual knows whether it is the Torah scroll itself that is being adored or the God represented by that scroll. The former borders on idolatry. The latter is the aim of Jewish spirituality.

We may ask, "Why was Judaism born at all? Why were Jews dissatisfied with idolatry as a paradigm?" We might also ask, "What, specifically, was lacking in Mesopotamian idolatry?" (Abraham, the founder of Judaism, had Mesopotamian roots.) Nahum Sarna (1966), in his commentary on the book of Genesis, outlines why idolatry might have been unsatisfactory to idolaters themselves:

The pagan worshiper had no reason to believe that the decrees of his god must necessarily be just, any more than he could be convinced that society rested upon a universal order of justice. According to the pagan world-view the fate of man was not determined by human behavior. The gods were innately capricious, so that any absolute authority was impossible. . . . Man always found himself confronted by the tremendous forces of nature, and nature, especially in Mesopotamia, showed itself to be cruel, indiscriminate, unpredictable. Since the gods were immanent in nature, they too shared these same harsh attributes. To aggravate the situation still further, there was always that inscrutable, primordial power beyond the realm of the gods to which man and gods were both subject. Evil, then, was a permanent necessity and there was nothing essentially good in the pagan universe. In such circumstances there could be no correlation between right conduct and individual or national well-being. The universe was purposeless and the deities could offer their votaries no guarantee that life had meaning and direction, no assurance that the end of human strivings was anything but vanity. [p. 17]

As we will see when we examine the way Judaism formulated the Jew's relationship to God, this problem created by Mesopotamian pagan theology is addressed head on. The Jewish God is as bound by the covenant as is the human being. Thus, the Jewish God, though omnipotent, allows the Divine power to be limited by the agreement the Deity entered into with the Jewish people. This is a remarkable sacrifice on the part of God and should engender great loyalty on the part of the Jews who benefit from this agreement.

Idolatry was, of course, practiced in other cultures besides Mesopotamia. For example, Roman and Greek gods were served in solemn, yet joyful, rituals. Sacrificial animals were offered up and the smoke went to the gods while the celebrants ate the animal's flesh. "Scraps from the meal were left on the altar and beggars spirited them away. When sacrifice was made not on a household altar but at a temple, the custom was to pay for the priests' services by leaving them a set portion of the sacrificial animal; temples earned money by selling this meat to butchers" (Aries and Duby 1987, 196). Judaism adapted many of these idolatrous rites in the Temple service to God. The paganism that surrounded Judaism was likely the impetus for its very creation and part of the template from which its theology and service were adapted.

### Judaism's Answer to Idolatry

The relationship between Jews and God can be conceived of as a marital bond. It is all about responsibility in the context of a relationship, the very opposite of the capricious, unreliable Mesopotamian gods. For example, if Jews keep the commandments, God will reward us. If we transgress them, God will punish us. This is clearly stated in the Torah:

> And it shall come to pass, if you shall hearken diligently unto My commandments which I command You this day, to love the Lord your God, and to serve Him with all your heart and with all your soul that I will give the rain of your land in its season, the former rain and the later rain, that you may gather in your corn and your wine and your oil. And I will give grass in your fields for your cattle and you shall eat and be satisfied. Take heed to yourselves lest your heart be deceived and you turn aside and serve other gods and worship them and the anger of the Lord be kindled against you and He shut up the heaven so that there shall be no rain and the ground shall not yield her fruit and you perish quickly from off the good land which the Lord gives you. [Deuteronomy 11:13–17]

It's a reliable, reasonable system. While this passage is the middle paragraph of the Shema, which is recited twice daily and is thus quite well known, we could easily find scores of similar passages in the Torah.

Remarkably, it is not just human beings who are bound by the mitzvot. Even God adheres to them:

> Rav Nachman bar Yitschak said to Rav Hiyya bar Avin: What is written in the tefillin of the Lord of the Universe? He replied to him: "And who is like Your people Israel, a nation unique in the earth?" (I Chronicles 17:21) Does then the Holy One, blessed be He, sing the praises of Israel? Yes. For it is written, "You have affirmed the Lord this day . . . and the Lord has affirmed you this day." (Deuteronomy 26:17, 18)
>
> The Holy One, blessed be He, said to Israel: You have made me a single entity in the world, and I shall make you a single entity in the world. "You have made me a single entity in the world," as it is said, "Hear O Israel, the Lord our God, the Lord is one." (Deuteronomy 6:4) "And I shall make you a single entity in the world," as it is said, "And who is like Your people Israel, a nation unique in the earth?" (I Chronicles 17:21) (*B. Berachot 6a*)

The tefillin are a symbol of the marital relationship between God and Israel. Every time a Jewish congregation says the Sanctification of God's name ("*kadosh, kadosh, kadosh*" [Isaiah 6:3]) they are reaffirming this bond. (The root of the word *kadosh, kuf-dalet-shin*, is used to describe a wedding, *kiddushin*.)

Part of a marital bond is a sense of ownership and its attendant jealousy. Halbertal and Margalit (1992) note that,

> Jealousy has two sides. One is a threat to the jealous person's power, in which case a person is not jealous of another unless his own self-esteem has been undermined by his rival's achievements. . . . The other side of jealousy is humiliation. When a wife leaves her husband for a nonentity, there is no real threat, but there is a very deep sense of humiliation. [p. 27]

But God can be wounded by idolatry not only as "husband" to "wife Israel." God can also be hurt by idolatry because it challenges God's position as the one true king:

> The sin represents a crisis in a political system. The political model provides us with a different understanding of the sin of idolatry. Instead of whoredom and nymphomania, instead of the forgetful woman who loses her identity, it uses the image of a rebellious slave who becomes a pretender to the throne when he is driven insane by jealousy and a craving for power. [p. 222]

So, Scripture and rabbinic literature variously depict idolatry as stupid (following one's eyes; worshiping things that can be seen, such as the sun, instead of the Creator of the universe), wanton (the marital model desecrated), or traitorous (the rebellious slave). To be a faithful Jew, one must see with clear vision and not let the obvious obscure that vision; one must be faithful and one must recognize the single, true source of ultimate power that voluntarily binds itself through a relationship with a people: God.

### This Tractate's Structure

Tractate *Avodah Zarah* is the volume of rabbinic literature that deals with Judaism's response to idolatry most thoroughly.

How is this tractate organized? The Mishnah and Gemara in this tractate take different approaches to the topic under discussion. The Mishnah, in its methodical, precise way, moves from the core of the encounter with idolatry to its periphery. The first chapter of the Mishnah concerns idolatrous people at idolatrous times (i.e., their holidays). The second chapter deals with idolatrous people in everyday situations. The third chapter shows how to deal with idols themselves and pieces thereof. The fourth chapter demonstrates how to deal with things associated with idols and idol worship. The fourth chapter also begins the examination of idolaters' wine, and this examination is extended into the fifth chapter. The wine of idolaters is ideal for exploring economic involvement with non-Jews because it can be the movable, imbibable, salable essence of idolatry. The movement of the Mishnah from core to periphery is demonstrated in Figure I–1.

The structure of the Mishnah is clear and logical: it moves systematically from the core to the periphery. The Gemara, as commentary to the Mishnah, does not follow the Mishnah's structure. Rather, the Gemara consistently focuses on inner states as the true test of whether idolatry is taking place. What interests the Gemara, if one could put it so broadly, is what is happening in a person's soul. Whether the issue is actual participation in idolatry or the smallest, most mundane moments of contact between Jew and idolater, the Gemara wants to elucidate what is happening inside a person.

This points to an essential difference between these two documents. The Mishnah is concerned with concrete, measurable phenomena. It is precise and materialistic in the sense that it expresses things through physical material. The Gemara here is more interested in expressing the same concepts as the Mishnah through intellectual and spiritual constructs. Thus, for example, in our very first mishnah, the economic relationship between Jews and idolaters during an idolatrous holiday is examined. The Gemara to this mishnah immediately comments on the spiritual consequences of idolatry, shifting the focus away from the Mishnah's measurable phenomena. As the tractate begins, and the Mishnah is dealing with relatively more spiritual issues, the Gemara's and the Mishnah's concerns are actually rather

**FIGURE I–1.**

closely linked. As the tractate moves on, however, the Gemara's interests remain steady and the Mishnah moves ever outward, and so the two documents increasingly take divergent paths. These two paths can help the contemporary reader "triangulate" his or her current concerns by using both approaches, the concrete and the spiritual, to determine a course for living an authentically Jewish life in a non-Jewish world.

## How to Use What Is in this Tractate Today

During the 1990s, the Jewish community has become consumed by the issue of "continuity." This problem was brought to light when a major survey demonstrated that, if present rates of assimilation prevail, the Jewish people will cease to exist in America in a rather short span of time (CJF 1991). Some readers of this book may be tempted to look to tractate *Avodah Zarah* for answers to this current-day problem. This may be a good strategy. In the first place, it means one's discussions will be based on Jewish texts, and this is almost always a good starting point. Second, it might open the eyes of today's policy-makers to strategies that have worked in the past, and it might make those leaders feel less alone, knowing that previous generations faced the same issues.

However, there are some pitfalls to be aware of if this is the reason one is studying tractate *Avodah Zarah*. When contemporary Jews see the term "non-Jew" we tend to think of Christians or followers of Islam. This would be a serious error. While some commentators considered Christians idolaters because of their belief in the Trinity and the incarnation of God, others, most notably R. Menahem Ha-Meiri (Katz 1961, 114–128), redefine Christianity as nonidolatrous because of the morally upright lifestyle that accompanies its practice. Katz's book is an excellent, easy-to-read, concise summary of how Jewish attitudes toward idolaters, Christians and followers of Islam have changed over time. When studying this topic it is even more important than usual to clearly understand the changes that occurred in different historical eras and the way attitudes varied even within eras.

At the risk of belaboring the point, let us be very clear at the outset: *when rabbinic literature speaks of non-Jews it is generally referring to idol worshipers, not to followers of Christianity or Islam.* We will occasionally compare predicaments ancient Jews faced with those of contemporary Jews who live in a Christian society. The risks Jews faced in living in an idolatrous milieu have some similarities to those Jews face today living in a Christian culture. But this does not mean that Jews today, nor this author certainly, view Christianity or Islam as the equivalents of idolatry.

### The Five Major Works of Rabbinic Literature

Rabbinic literature is made up of five major works, each of which has its own characteristic traits. Because all five sources of material will appear in this volume, a brief introduction to each of them is in order. The five main works are (1) the Mishnah, (2) the *Tosefta*, (3) the Talmud of the Land of Israel (the *Yerushalmi*), (4) the Midrash collections, and (5) the Talmud of Babylonia (the *Bavli*). Those parts of the Talmuds that are commentary on the Mishnah are called Gemara. The term "Talmud" refers to the Mishnah and Gemara combined.

Rabbinic literature is frequently called the Oral Torah. Tradition has it that God whispered the laws and customs contained in the Oral Torah to Moses on Mount Sinai at the same time God gave Moses the Written Torah (the first five books of the Bible). This Oral Torah was passed down through the generations, "from Moses to Joshua; Joshua to the elders; the elders to the prophets" (*M. Pirkei Avot* 1:1). Many scholars believe that these teachings of the Oral Torah developed during a much later period. Regardless of the time of its genesis, the Oral Torah was the sages' method of making the Written Torah meaningful to the people of their day. Table I–1 summarizes some important historical information about the different works of rabbinic literature and the abbreviations we will use, with the name of the tractates, or individual books of the Oral Torah, to identify this material

**Table I–1**

| Work | Date Finished | Place Finished | Abbreviation |
|------|--------------|----------------|--------------|
| Mishnah | 200 C.E. | The Land of Israel | M.+ tractate name |
| *Tosefta* | 220–230 C.E. | The Land of Israel | T.+ tractate name |
| *Yerushalmi* | 400 C.E. | The Land of Israel | Y.+ tractate name |
| Midrash | 400–500 C.E. | The Land of Israel | full name used |
| *Bavli* | 427–520 C.E. | Babylonia | B.+ tractate name |

## These Five Works as "People"

How do these five different kinds of rabbinic literature differ from each other? In general, the Mishnah, which was compiled first, contains an outline of how the law given in the written Torah is to be followed. It is more theoretical than practical. Practical details are provided by the *Tosefta, Yerushalmi* and the *Bavli*. The Midrash collections are unique in that they are made up principally of stories that expound biblical passages rather than focusing primarily on Jewish law and practice.

One way to understand the interrelationship of these rabbinic writings is to think about them as different personality types. Mishnah is like a dreamer who's always imagining how things should be rather than thinking about how they are. This sort of person is always concocting beautiful schemes to organize her life. The only problem is that these dreams don't necessarily relate to reality.

*Tosefta* is like the Mishnah's more practical friend. When the Mishnah goes off on an idealistic tangent, *Tosefta* says, "Wait a minute. I don't think that's going to work the way you think it's going to. And what if conditions change? And have you thought of all the consequences?"

The *Yerushalmi* is like *Tosefta*, only more so. The *Yerushalmi* listens to the Mishnah and *Tosefta* and then takes over the conversation, citing statistics and information from a vast library of knowledge. The *Yerushalmi* may take a long time to come to a decision, but usually it will eventually tell you that, "Yes, the Mishnah's plan will work" or "No, the Mishnah's plan won't work, but *Tosefta*'s might" or "Neither the Mishnah nor the

*Tosefta* have it right. However, I have an answer that I've dug up which I think *will* work."

The Midrash collections, which comment on different books of the Bible rather than on the Mishnah, as does the rest of rabbinic literature, are loners. They're loosely connected to the Mishnah, *Tosefta*, *Yerushalmi*, and *Bavli*, but they really go their own way. They're like that one member of a circle of friends who is included, but not terribly attached. And are they into telling stories! The difference between the Mishnah and the Midrash collections is that the Mishnah wants to pretend that her dreams are going to shape reality. The Midrash collections want to tell stories and find meaning and enjoyment in life without necessarily legislating that vision. It's sort of like the difference between a politician (the Mishnah) and a political commentator (the Midrash collections): one is into prescribing solutions and the other is into talking about problems and brainstorming ideas.

Finally, the *Bavli* is like the *Yerushalmi* . . . and not like the *Yerushalmi*. Like the *Yerushalmi*, the *Bavli* listens to the Mishnah and *Tosefta* and then takes over the conversation. However, unlike the *Yerushalmi*, the *Bavli* isn't so "bottom line" oriented. The *Bavli* is more interested in exploring options than in determining the one right solution to a problem. Also, the *Bavli* loves to tell stories; almost as much as the Midrash collections do. Finally, the *Bavli* is a bit more talkative than the *Yersuhalmi*—who was already quite talkative.

If you ever gathered these five "people" in a room, the Mishnah would start the conversation, next *Tosefta* would get in a few comments, then the conversation would be taken over by the *Yerushalmi* and the *Bavli*. The Midrash collections would be over in a corner studying Torah and occasionally contributing to the conversation.

We will naturally be focusing on the *Bavli* in this book, but part of the goal in this third volume of *The Talmud for Beginners* is to move the reader beyond the *Bavli*, so passages from *Tosefta*, Midrash, and the *Yerushalmi* will also be cited as we move through our material.

### Some Notes on Style and Translations

A few words should be said about the style used in this book. Indented passages are selections from the *Tanach* (the Jewish Bible) or rabbinic literature. *Bavli* passages are cited according to their traditional folio numbers from the Vilna edition, and passages from the *Yerushalmi* are cited according to the Venice Edition. When a passage is cited in more than one place within rabbinic literature, these parallel passages will be noted with the symbol "//" plus the name of the work and the page number on which it appears. The word Mishnah with a capital "M" indicates the entire work: all six tractates. The word mishnah with a lower case "m" indicates one small passage from that work.

The translations of rabbinic literature used in this book are adapted from the Soncino translations of the Mishnah, *Bavli* and *Midrash Rabbah*, Jacob Neusner's translations of *Tosefta* and the *Yerushalmi*, Hammer's translation of Sifre to Deuteronomy, and Lauterbach's translation of *Mekhilta*. Although gender-inclusive language is used in the text, the translations reflect that the language used to describe God in rabbinic literature is most often in the male gender.

# 1

# Exploring the Heart of Judaism

I studied in the Soviet Union for a semester many years ago, when the Soviet Union still existed and Leningrad had not yet reverted to its original name of Saint Petersburg. For weeks, I was able to watch as tanks and missile-bearing trucks rolled by our dorm at night on their way to practice for the big October Revolution parade on the main square of the city. The parade was electric. Endless crowds. Miles of placards and banners, all proclaiming the hope that communism would triumph and that capitalism would be defeated by the tanks, missiles, and soldiers so precisely displayed. This capitalist, at the very least, felt quite small and vulnerable when confronted with that power and the fervor with which it was supported. Of course, I also knew that people *had* to be at the parade and that, as obviously became manifest in subsequent years, most of them actually wanted to be capitalists.

## The Heart of Idolatry

That feeling of being overwhelmed and vulnerable, yet knowing in your heart that your way of life is truly good, even though other people are bent on eradicating it, is where this tractate begins. The sages consider how one should relate to idol worshipers during their most intensely idolatrous times. As it often does, the Mishnah focuses on this issue by using easily quantified commercial relationships as its angle of approach:

3

**MISHNAH (2a):** [For] three days before the festivities (אידיהן *eideihen*) of idolaters [literally, "star worshipers'], it is forbidden to transact business with them; to lend [to them] and to borrow from them; to lend [money] to them and to borrow [money] from them; to repay money [to them] or to accept repayment from them. Rabbi Yehudah says: We accept repayment from them, because this depresses them. [The sages] said to him: Even though it depresses them now, it makes them happy later.

**GEMARA:** Rav and Samuel [differed]: the one quoting [from this Mishnah] אידיהן *edeihen*, while the other quoted עידיהן *'eideihen*. The one who quoted *eideihen* is not in error, nor is the one who quoted עידיהן *'eideihen* in error.

The one who quoted אידיהן *eideihen* is not in error, since it is written [in Scripture]: "For the day of their calamity [אידם *eidam*] is at hand" (Deuteronomy 32:35). And the one who quotes עידיהן *'eideihen* not in error, for it is written [in Scripture]: "Let them bring their witnesses [testimonies, עידיהם *'edeihem*] that they may be justified" (Isaiah 43:9).

And the one who quotes אידיהן *eideihen*, why doesn't he teach עידיהן *'eideihen*? He might say, the term אידיהן *eideihen* ["calamity"] is more applicable [to idolatry]. And the one who quotes עידיהן *'eideihen*, why does he not teach *eideihen*? He might say: What is it that brings about their calamity if not the testimony [with which] they testify against themselves. Hence the term עדות *'eidut* ["testimony"] is more fitting.

Let us first examine the mishnah, and then the Gemara's commentary on it. The mishnah is a straightforward dictate of etiquette and economics. If idolaters and idolatry are the enemy, then transacting business with them three days before their holidays, i.e., when their idolatry is at its most intense, will only aid the enemy. The money a Jew hands over to them will enable the idolaters to celebrate their idolatry even better, since they're likely to take the money they make from a transaction with a Jew and use it to buy libations for their gods. It would be like buying things from the store of a Klansman three days before a large KKK rally. Your money might then purchase the gasoline they'd use to start a fire. Therefore, the sages mandate that no business be done with idolaters, "the enemy," three days before their festivals, so that Jewish money might not contribute to the loathsome proceedings.

Why exactly three days? The *Yerushalmi* to this mishnah says that the idolaters in Babylonia only took one day to prepare for their festival. (We note that in *B. Hullin* 13b, Rabbi Hiyya bar Abba says in the name of Rabbi Yohanan that non-Jews outside the Land of Israel are not idolaters and are merely continuing the customs of their ancestors. As early as the layer of the Gemara, then, there seems to be a tendency, on a practical level, to moderate the Mishnah's harsh pronouncements that might make economic life untenable in the Diaspora.) In the Land of Israel, however, it appears that the idolaters prepared for three days, and so business dealings with them were cut off for that time period. Alternatively, the ban against such business dealings may have been more easily enforced there, and so it was maintained. Depending on the number of such festivals, and depending on how strictly the public adhered to the Mishnah's teachings, this might represent a considerable inconvenience and financial disadvantage. Like Jews of any age, some people probably observed these rules to the letter, and many probably did not, ranging from basic compliance to outright defiance. This is like a boycott on lettuce or grapes conducted out of protest for the way the workers who harvest these goods are treated. If a boycott is widely adhered to, it can have a significant economic impact. So, too, this doctrine might have greatly limited economic interaction between Jews and non-Jews.

The way the Gemara responds to this mishnah sets the tone for the creative tension between these two documents that will resonate throughout the entire tractate. Instead of focusing on the Mishnah's issue of concrete economic interaction, the Gemara immediately latches on to the internal state that leads idolaters into the error of idolatry. The Gemara puzzles over, and makes puns on, the word *ed*. This word is used infrequently in the Mishnah and, in fact, is used only in this tractate. The usual term for holiday is *chag*, but it is not used here. It may be that the sages did not want to dignify idolatrous holidays by giving them the same name used for Jewish festivals. For example, we would probably not call a KKK rally or a Soviet October

Revolution march a High Holiday, even though these events might be as important to these groups as the Days of Awe are to us.

There seems to be a difference of opinion between Rav and Shmuel as to how this word designating a pagan festival is spelled. One holds that it is spelled with an *aleph*, the other that it is spelled with an *ayin*. The rest of this passage is most likely a later commentary that provides reasons for Rav and Shmuel's difference of opinion. Like many similar passages in the Gemara, it is anonymous and provides justification for two different points of view. Both opinions are regarded as valid. This reflects the Gemara's philosophy that the truth is such an enormous entity that it is capable of containing within itself apparently opposing viewpoints while remaining logically consistent. This is characteristic of the later layer of the Talmud, which is the work of the *stamma*, or the anonymous editor of the Talmud. Sometimes it helps for the beginning student to see these anonymous, usually somewhat difficult sections as footnotes that found their way into the text. Read them as you would footnotes: not analyzing them as you would the text but almost skimming them for important information. How can you identify these "footnote" sections? They generally don't cite named sources and they have a certain quality, a sort of see-saw, make-everything-harmonize drive behind them that, once identified, can be picked up quite consistently. For example, in this passage, everyone's opinion is justified and the anonymous composer of the passage can see the issue from every participant's point of view.

The prooftexts used to affirm the alternative spellings of this word were evidently chosen with care. Deuteronomy 32 is Moses' last song to the Children of Israel. Verse 35 speaks of God's power to punish misdeeds:

To Me belongs vengeance, and recompense,
when their foot slides:
for the day of their calamity (אידם *edam, aleph-yud-dalet-mem*)
    is at hand,
and the things that shall come upon them make haste.

Here, *ed* means "calamity." Though it used elsewhere in the *Tanach*, this is the only time it is used in the Torah.

The other spelling of the word עד *'ed*, with an ע *ayin*, means witness, and in Isaiah is part of a passage calling on Israel to be witnesses to God's oneness and power.

> Let all the nations be gathered together, and let the peoples be assembled: who among them can declare this, and announce to us former things? Let them bring forth their witnesses (עידיהם *'eideihem*), that they may be justified: or let them hear, and say, It is truth. [Isaiah 43:9]

In one instance the word *eid* means calamity, which gives a fitting overtone to the concept of a pagan holiday. In the other instance, *'eid* refers to acting as a witness for one's deity. Both ways of spelling the word can be used to give a negative meaning to idolatrous goings-on, and so both are validated.

Note that the Gemara here is basically ignoring the mishnah's agenda. In fact, this introductory passage will lead into the topic that really concerns the Gemara: the outlining of monotheism's supremacy over idolatry; the ways in which God is just and all-powerful, even when facts would appear to the contrary; and the ways in which God's system of rewards and punishments work.

## Torah: Receiving It and Its Reward

In the years when the Gemara was composed, 200–500 C.E., the sages were compelled to explain to their constituents how the inner faithful relationship between God and the Jewish people was triumphing even as it appeared that paganism was winning. The sages envisioned the glorious day when this would be revealed and their wisdom, and the idolaters' foolishness, will be exposed for all to see:

> **GEMARA (2a):** In the time to come, the Holy One, blessed be He, will take a scroll of the Torah in His embrace and say: "Let him who has occupied himself herewith come and take his reward." Immediately all the nations will crowd together in

confusion, as it is said: "All the nations are gathered together" (Isaiah 43:9). The Holy One, blessed be He, will say to them: "Enter before Me in confusion. Rather, let each nation come in (2b) with its scribes." . . . Immediately the Kingdom of Rome (Edom) will enter first before Him. . . . The Holy One, blessed be He, will say to them: "With what have you occupied yourselves?" They will say before Him: "Master of the World, we have established many marketplaces, we have erected many baths, we have accumulated much silver and gold, and all this we did only for the sake of Israel, that they might [have leisure] for occupying themselves with the study of Torah." The Holy One, blessed be He, will say to them: "[You are the biggest] fools in the world! All that you have done, [you have only done] to satisfy your own desires. You have established marketplaces to place prostitutes therein; baths, to revel in them; [as to the distribution of] silver and gold, that is Mine, as it is written: 'Mine is the silver and Mine is the gold, says the Lord of Hosts.'" (*Haggai* 2:8).

Are there any among you who have been declaring "this"? As it is said, "Who among you can say this (*zot*)? (Isaiah 43:9) And "this" is nothing else than the Torah, as it is said: "And *this* (*v'zot*) is the Law (*haTorah*) which Moses set [before the children of Israel]" (Deuteronomy 4:44). They will then depart crushed in spirit. On the departure of the Kingdom of Rome, Persia will enter after her.

The exposition of the passage from Isaiah (43:9–10) continues in this passage as the nations' "testimony" brings about their "calamity" at God's ultimate trial of judgment. What an image of God! There God stands with Torah in hand, a physical aspect, identified with Israel body and soul, as it were, judging the nations for their lack of devotion to Torah. God is the prosecutor, judge, and jury in this vision, forcing Edom to face its true self. God here is both the universal Deity of every nation and the special God of Israel. This is yet another example of the way that rabbinic literature can contain within it what appear to be conflicting parts of the truth. On the one hand, the sages hold that God is incorporeal. On the other hand, God can have a physical presence, as in this story. God is the God of all the universe. And God has a special relationship with Israel. All these statements are true for the sages.

Edom is another name the sages used for Rome. In the first centuries of the Common Era, Jews had to explain to themselves how it could be that Roman idolatry had triumphed while Judaism had apparently been conquered. Rome is portrayed as cowering and deceitful in this reckoning at the end of time. The Romans try to convince God that they did everything for the benefit of the Jewish people; in order to foster their study of Torah. God, of course, is not fooled and brands them as mindless sensualists. The contrast is plain: Jews are a people of book and mind; Romans are a people of the flesh. The Persians are likewise condemned by God for building bridges, conquering cities, and waging war. In other words, the mighty nations that appear triumphant in contemporary history will be defeated by Israel at the end of time. So, the sages seem to tell us, what looks like defeat is really only a temporary low point before the final glorious conclusion of the story. We can easily imagine that this sort of scenario would comfort Jews who felt defeated and longed for a time of religious and political independence and popularity for their faith and people. This passage shows us the sages' frame of mind: they feel defeated by mighty forces and search for comfort in projections of the ultimate triumph over their enemies.

This is a frame of mind that is probably very difficult for most Americans to step into. We have been almost uniformly successful in war and have managed to influence distant countries through the export of our culture. Our nation is vast and has rarely been invaded. Contrast this with the sages' situation when they lived in the Land of Israel. They dwelt in a small country that was repeatedly invaded and whose culture was rejected by the conqueror. This situation is more like that of Lithuania, for example, under Soviet rule. The joy with which Lithuanians threw off the Soviet yoke, and all the cultural manifestations that went with it, such as the Russian language, are echoed in this passage as the sages envision throwing off the rule of earthly tyrants. As Americans, we might feel that the sages gloat too much in this story. Yet, if we can place ourselves in their position, we can see they are performing a vital task: assuring Jews that there is a reason to stay Jewish. They will be able to practice their Judaism in freedom and pride one day in the future. The sages are much like the Lithuanian nationalists who insisted on keeping their heritage and language alive during the period of Soviet domination.

The source of this future glory, as is the case in almost all rabbinic visions of history, stems from the Torah. In general, the sages tie every holiday and every significant event in Jewish history back to the era of the Torah. For example, the fast commemorating the breaching of Jerusalem's walls on the Seventeenth of Tammuz begins with the "cosmic wound," as it were, of the breaking of the Tablets, which was also said to have happened on that date. Likewise, the destruction of the Temple on the Ninth of Av was presaged by the Israelite's refusal to enter the Land and God's decree against them on that date (*M. Taanit* 4:6). So, in this tractate, Israel's ultimate redemption is linked to the Toraitic event of their having accepted the law. God will similarly call the nations of the world to task for having failed to accept it.

> **GEMARA (2b):** The Holy One, blessed be He, offered the Torah to every nation and every tongue, but none accepted it, until He came to Israel who accepted it. [The nations will defend their rejection of Torah in the following way.] They will say thus: "Did we accept it and fail to observe it?" But surely the obvious rejoinder [to their plea] would be: "Why did you not accept it?" Then they will say thus before Him: "Master of the World, did You suspend the mountain over us like a vault, as You have done to Israel and did we still decline to accept it?" For it is written: "And they stood at the nether part (תחתית *tachtit*) of the mountain" (Exodus 19:17). Rav Dimi bar Hama said: This teaches that the Holy One, blessed be He, suspended the mountain over Israel like a vault, and said unto them: "If you accept the Torah, it will be well with you, but if not, there will be your grave."

If Torah is, as the sages fully believed, the self-evident truth and word of God, then why can't everyone see that? Why do the powerful nations of the world reject it? The sages here imagine that at the end of time these nations will be called to account for their blindness. They, in turn, will point a finger at the Jews and say, "Look, at least we aren't as bad as Jews who had the Torah and failed to follow it!" But this line of reasoning will not do them any good since God will remind them that they had the chance to accept Torah and did not take advantage of it. Indeed, there are many stories in rabbinic literature about how God offered the Torah to everyone. For example, this is one of the reasons why Torah was given in the open, at Mount Sinai, rather than in the Land of Israel, so that everyone who wished to could come and receive it (*Mekhilta d'Rabbi Yishmael, Bachodesh* 5 on Exodus 20:2). The nations will respond with the sages' story that God had to hold Mount Sinai over the Jewish people and threaten to drop the very mountain on them before they would accept the Torah. The word *tachtit,* "nether part," caught the sages' attention: it is rarely used in Hebrew Scripture. Therefore, the sages assumed it must be a very special sort of "nether part" to be denoted with this word. It couldn't simply be the foot of the mountain, so they envisioned it as the mountain's underside, which the Israelites viewed from the perspective of being directly beneath it. (One interpretation we could give this midrash is that God presents the alternatives at Sinai as Torah or death. Perhaps this is the sages' way of saying that life without Torah is like death.)

The nations, in this scenario, point to a truth we may not want to acknowledge: there have always been Jews who have resisted Torah and have had to be more, or less, forcibly reminded of its role in their lives. Were Jews then so different from Jews now? What does it take to make Jews really accept Torah, for them to learn it and practice it? Can you coerce someone into observing Judaism? God apparently had to coerce the Israelites. Then the Israelites rebelled, made the golden calf, and ended up wandering in the desert for forty years. The coercion was not terribly effective. On the other hand, converts to Judaism, who had (ideally) no taint of coercion on themselves or on their ancestors, who experienced neither the parting of the Red Sea nor the dramatic display of smoke and fire at Mount Sinai, are held to be meritorious compared to the Jews who worshiped the golden calf:

> Who were they that despised the Omnipresent? They were the worshipers of the calf. What disgrace did He inflict on them? They were smitten with leprosy and with gonorrhea and He sent

them out of the camp; for it says, "that they put out of the camp every leper" (Numbers 5:2).

What honor did the Holy One, blessed be He, confer upon the proselytes? That after the section [concerning] the removal of unclean [persons], the [section containing the] caution regarding proselytes is written. It teaches you that the Omnipresent kept the sinners of Israel at a distance and He brought close to Him the proselytes who came for the sake of His name, for He made their suit as important as that of Israel, for anyone that robs them, it is as if he robbed an Israelite. This explains the text, "For them that honor Me I will honor" (I Samuel 2:30). [*Bamidbar Rabbah* 8:3]

The verse from I Samuel outlines Divine faithfulness, reciprocity, and consistency: "For those that honor Me will I honor and those that despise Me shall be lightly esteemed" (I Samuel 2:30). The sin of leprosy is often associated with moral guilt (see, for example, *B. Arakhin* 15b–16a), such as speaking evilly about another person. Those who worshiped the golden calf became lepers and were therefore banished from the community. The proselytes, on the other hand, were honored by God because they had honored God. Converts are the equals of born Jews under the law (i.e., they have parity in the laws of robbery) and are the betters of Jews who betray their faith, for example, by worshiping the golden calf. One lesson we can draw from this scenario is that a relationship based solely on bedazzling one party with drama and coercing them with power doesn't work. In some ways, it has the taint of idolatry on it since it uses power outside of a mutually agreed to relationship that would serve as the framework for the exercise of power. Perhaps the worship of the golden calf was the logical outcome of the Israelites having had Mount Sinai held over their heads.

In the end, of course, the nations of the world did not accept the Torah. However, this did not mean that they were left out of God's system of law. No, non-Jews need only follow the "Noahide commandments," the laws given to humanity before there were any Jews or laws for Jews. These laws prohibit everyone from practicing idolatry, blasphemy, bloodshed, sexual sins (e.g., incest), theft, and eating from a living animal. In addition, legal systems must be established (*T. Avodah Zarah* 8:4).

In other words, all a non-Jew must do to achieve redemption in the World to Come is behave like a *mensch*, while Jews must observe the 613 commandments. In some ways, this doesn't seem fair: it's easier to achieve redemption as a non-Jew than as a Jew, and the sages are quick to point this out.

> **GEMARA (2b):** For Rav Yosef learned (*B. Baba Kamma* 38a): "He stands and shakes the earth, He sees and makes the nations tremble" (Habakuk 3:6). What did He see? He saw that the nations did not observe [even] the seven precepts that the sons of Noah had taken upon themselves, and seeing that they did not observe them, He stood up and released them therefrom. Then they benefited by it. According to this it pays to be a sinner!— Said Mar bar Ravina: (3a) The release from those commands only means that even if they observed them they would not receive a reward. [Why] not? Is it not taught: Rabbi Meir used to say, "Whence do we know that even a star worshiper who studies the Torah is equal to a High Priest? Scripture says: '[You shall therefore keep My statutes and My ordinances which,] if a person (*ha'adam*) do, he shall live by them' (Leviticus 18:5). It is not said, 'If Priests, Levites, and Israelites do,' but 'a person.' Thus you learn that even a star worshiper who studies the Torah is equal to a High Priest!" Rather, it comes to teach you that they do not receive the reward that [those who are] commanded [to do a mitzvah] and perform [it] receive. [Rather] they are like one who is not commanded [to do a mitzvah] and does it, as Rabbi Hanina said: He who is commanded and does [a mitzvah], is greater than he who is not commanded [to do a mitzvah] and does it.

Before we analyze this passage, note how the Gemara is once more focusing on internal states. The power of Torah study causes even the most critical external differences between people (e.g., one's lineage, which was extremely important in ancient days) to fall away. Torah transforms people from the inside out and renders an idolater the equal of a High Priest! Torah's power can change people, their status, and their relationships.

The sages first ask about the verse from Habbakuk, "What did God see that then made the nations tremble?" What God saw was that these nations could not even keep the seven

Noachide commandments, so God basically cut them off immediately and didn't even obligate them to perform those seven
commandments. But did the nations experience this dispensa-
tion as a reward? No. Being released from the obligation to
perform these seven precepts meant that, even if they should
reform and do them, they would not receive the reward for
them. But an objection is raised, "You mean that performing
these commandments, whether one is obligated to do them or
not, has no merit and no reward? That hardly seems fair!"
Indeed, if we think of the nations as a criminal who, after being
sentenced to life in prison without possibility of parole, reforms
and begins to behave well, we would imagine that this ought to
count for something. Not that this good behavior will mitigate
the past crime or reduce the sentence, but it probably would
earn the prisoner some sort of reward within the prison environment. The sages, who are usually quite generous in accepting
the power of repentance, show no such inclination in this
passage. These same sages composed the following passage
about the power of penitence:

> Rabbi Abbahu said, "In the place where penitents stand even
> the wholly righteous cannot stand, as it says, 'Pease, peace to him
> that was far and to him that is near.' (Isaiah 57:19)—to him that
> was far first, and then to him that is near." [*B. Berachot* 34b]

Yet, in the case of the nations, the sages are inclined to be
harsh. Why? First of all, there is a difference between an
individual and a nation. Second, this whole passage focuses on
the final judgment at the end of days. The sages, who feel so
beleaguered in the present, achieve relief and healing contemplating the eventual rendering of strict justice against those who
oppressed the Jews for so long and appeared to triumph.

Rabbi Meir's teaching about the equalizing power of Torah
study is brought in support of the nations, to balance this desire
for judgment. Commenting on the way the Torah phrases the
command to study Torah and live by its precepts, he notes that
each person is promised this reward, not only Jews. Torah study
demolishes the difference between Jew and non-Jew, man and
woman, high-born and low-born. A society based on Torah

study is democratic: wealth, position, or birth are erased as factors, and a level playing field is established. There was no denying this basic teaching, which was axiomatic for the sages: their own power was based on their proficiency in Torah study. So how can we understand the assertion that the nations would not be rewarded for observing the Noachide commandments even after they were given an exemption from observing them? The Gemara makes a fine distinction using another well-known Jewish principle: a person who is obligated to do something is rewarded for doing it more than someone who is not so obligated. Therefore, the nations would be rewarded if they managed to perform these seven commandments, but not as greatly as would other peoples who were obligated to do them.

We can understand this basic principle through the following analogy. Let's say we have four people, A, B, C and D. A is owed money by B and C and will charge them a stiff penalty if they do not repay the money by five o'clock on a given day. D, who does not owe A money, offers to deliver the money for B and C. However, since D does not owe any money and does not fear any penalty, he may not feel the same sense of urgency to deliver the money on time as would B and C. B and C are obligated in this scenario and D is only trying to be helpful. It is not that D is incompetent or ill-willed, it is simply that D will not face the penalties for failure to repay the loan in a timely fashion, just as D did not reap the rewards of the borrowed funds. Just so are those who are obligated to observe the mitzvot rewarded differently for their observance than those who are not. Likewise, they are penalized for failing to observe the commandments, while those who are not obligated are not so penalized. This is counterintuitive: we would think that the volunteer would be rewarded more richly than the paid worker, so to speak. But the volunteer can walk away from his duties any time while the worker must be more reliable. Reliability is prized as the hallmark of the relationship between a person and God.

So the nations end up defeated according to this passage. Having once forsaken the most minimal obligations of humanity, they stand before God, trembling. Now, even if they perform these actions they will not gain the full reward for them. This is a further extension of the sages' triumphant scenario for the end of time: the Jews will triumph and the nations that oppressed them will be utterly crushed by God.

Will God enjoy this Divine judgment of the nations, finally putting them in the low place that they have earned for themselves? There is ambivalence about this in the Gemara. Some sages suggest that God has not laughed since the Temple was destroyed and will only laugh again on this day of final judgment. Others disagree, opining that God laughs every day:

> **GEMARA (3b):** Rav Yehudah said in the name of Rav: "The day consists of twelve hours. [In] the first three hours the Holy One, blessed be He, sits and studies Torah. [In] the second [three hours], He sits and judges the entire world. When He sees that the world is so guilty as to deserve destruction, He stands, covers the Judgment [seat], and sits on the Mercy Seat. [In] the third [period of three hours], He sits and feeds the entire world, from the horned buffalo to the brood of vermin. [In the] fourth [three hour period], He sits and plays with the leviathan, as it is said, "There is leviathan, whom You have formed to sport therewith" (Psalm 104:26).

What a fabulous role model for maintaining oneself spiritually and in one's relationships! If we were to imitate God we would spend one-quarter of our time studying Torah and spiritually nourishing ourselves, one-quarter of our time working to make the world a better place, one-quarter of our time tending to our families (for the creatures are God's family from the greatest animal—the buffalo—to the lowliest—the mouse) and one-quarter of our time relaxing and playing. If we cannot achieve that division each day, perhaps we can seek to achieve these proportions of activities over the course of our lifetimes.

The literary construction of this passage is marvelous. God sits, as befits a king, studying, judging, feeding, and playing. The only time God is portrayed as moving is when God shifts from an aspect of judgment to one of mercy. The sages conceived of this shift as so great that it necessarily entailed actual realignment on God's part. In the sages' literary style, the most important part of a story happens right in its center. God's movement from judgment to mercy is the most salient part of

God's day and, perhaps, the most miraculous evidence of Divine grace. Thus the moment of God's shifting from one attitude to another is placed at the heart of this passage.

This passage suggests that, while God may indeed rejoice at the judgment of the nations for their faithlessness at the end of time, this is not the only thing that makes God laugh with pleasure. If we think about our own lives, we can see the truth of this balanced view. We laugh and enjoy ourselves. However, when a long-standing injustice is righted, it is as if an annoying background hum that traced through our days is shut off and we feel a sense of peace and resolution. When the Berlin Wall came down, it was this sort of experience. An injustice that weighed on all humanity was righted, and everyone stood a little more proudly on that day. It is natural to rejoice when justice is done, and God experiences this, too.

Though God will judge the nations at the end of time, they will not be alone. Israel, too, will be judged. However, God will show mercy when punishing Israel because of the merit Israel has accrued by studying and practicing Torah. The following passage is but another in our long introductory section focusing on the eventual vindication of Judaism and contrasting it with the troubles of the contemporary Jewish community. Here, it is not an idolater that challenges Judaism but a *min*, that is, a Jew who has become a Christian.

**GEMARA (4a):** Rabbi Abbahu commended Rav Safra to the *minim* as a great[ly learned] man. Thus he was exempted by them from paying taxes for thirteen years. One day, on coming across him, they said to him: "It is written: 'You only have I known from all the families of the earth; therefore I will visit upon you all your iniquities' (Amos 3:2). If one is in anger one does not vent it on one's friend!?" He was silent and did not say [anything]. So they wound a scarf round his neck and tortured him. Rabbi Abbahu came and found him [in that state]. He said to them, "Why do you torture him?" Said they to him, "Did you not tell us that he is a great man? He cannot explain to us the meaning of this verse!" Said he, "I may have told you [that he was learned] in *Tannaitic* teaching; did I tell you [he was learned] in Scripture?" They said to him, "How is it that you know it?" He said to them, "We, who are frequently with you, set ourselves the task of studying it thoroughly, but others [i.e., from Babylonia] do not study it as carefully." Said they, "Tell us [the meaning of this verse]." He said to them, "I will explain it by a parable. To what may it be compared? To a man who is the creditor of two persons, one a friend and one an enemy. [From] his friend he will accept payment little by little whereas of his enemy he will exact payment in one moment!"

The *minim* granted Rav Safra a tax exemption for many years. However, when he was unable to answer one of their questions they tortured him since, perhaps, they felt they had been defrauded. Rabbi Abbahu rescues Rav Safra by appealing to the apparently well-known difference between sages in the Land of Israel and those from Babylonia: the former knew Scriptures better and the latter concentrated more on the Oral Torah. Babylonian sages never produced their own corpus of commentaries to biblical books. In fact, when Hillel first arrived in the Land of Israel from Babylonia, his teachings were based on reasoning rather than Scripture (*B. Pesachim* 66a), perhaps pointing to a long-standing difference between these two major centers in Jewish teaching.

It seems logical that Judaism would develop differently in different locales and emphasize those areas needed to deal with the local environment, much as an organism produces antibodies to the threats in its surroundings. Apparently, in the Land of Israel the sages needed to know Scripture more than Mishnah since they had to "fence" with more *minim*, while the sages of Babylonia could concentrate on the Mishnah as they did not face the same challenge. Obviously, Christians are more interested in Jewish Scripture, which they claim as their own, than in Mishnah and Gemara, to which they do not lay any claim. These different areas of emphasis have an interesting corollary today in American Jewish life. Those Jewish children who attend public school, and their parents, often spend a great deal of energy coping with the overwhelming Christian influences present in even the most sensitively run public school systems. Those children who attend Jewish day schools are free to understand their Jewish heritage, not in terms of answering questions from non-Jews, but on its own terms.

The explanation of the verse from Amos is clear. The verse itself is a bit strange. If God knows only us and, it is implied, loves us, why is God going to call us to account for all our sins? There is no question that God will fairly judge Jew and non-Jew for their sins. It is in the nature of their punishment that there will be a difference. The nations, who showed no fealty to God at all will be punished immediately, while Israel, who has shown loyalty to God—albeit imperfect—will only suffer the punishment bit by bit. Note that Abbahu's clever answer assures the *minim*, who he clearly sees as heretics, and the Jewish listener of God's great justice, which extends to everyone, as well as God's love and mercy for Israel.

We may, perhaps, empathize with Rav Safra. Who among us has not stood tongue-tied when confronted by members of another faith who say, "Explain this verse" or "Explain this Jewish custom"? Only the most encyclopedic knowledge of Jewish sources would allow a person to answer every such question "on one foot," as it were. Usually, we need to look up the verse and research the answer. (Of course, that's the key: knowing how to find the answer to a question, not necessarily knowing the answer. And how do you find the answer? Having a decent Jewish commentary to the Bible and/or the Encyclopedia Judaica in your home are good resources with which to start. Many Jewish resources are now available on CD-ROM. Some suggestions for your library are listed in the Bibliography.)

## The Power of Repentance and Torah

After these descriptions of God's stern justice, the sages balance the picture with a depiction of God's mercy in the face of the worst sorts of behavior. Here, as in many passages in rabbinic literature, idolatry is likened to adultery. We are in a marital relationship with God: one people owing loyalty to one God and to one God only. But just as a wayward spouse can be forgiven, so God forgives the Jewish people for their lapses into idolatry. One implication of this passage is that God could even forgive the nations if they would forsake idolatry. This is a classic example of the way the Gemara can voice opposing viewpoints with equal vigor. Above, we learned that the nations were well nigh unforgivable. Here, we learn that no one is beyond repentance and, therefore, forgiveness.

> **GEMARA (4b):** Rabbi Yehoshua ben Levi said: The Israelites made the [golden] calf only in order to give an opportunity to penitents [for them to believe in repentance's efficacy], as it is said, "O that they had such a heart as this always, to fear Me and keep all my commandments" (Deuteronomy 5:26). This last statement accords with what Rabbi Yohanan said in the name of Rabbi Shimon ben Yohai: David was not the kind [of man to do] that act [sleep with Bathsheba], nor was Israel the kind [of people to do] that act [worship the calf]. David was not the kind [of man to do] that act, as it is written, "My heart is slain within me" (Psalm 109:22); nor were the Israelites the kind [of people to do] that act, for it is said, "O that they had such a heart as this always [to fear Me, and keep all My commandments, that it might be well with them and with their children forever]" (Deuteronomy 5:26). Then why did they do [it]? (5a) To teach you that if an individual has sinned [and hesitates about the effect of repentance] he could be referred to the individual [who sinned and was forgiven, i.e., David], and if a community commit a sin they should be referred to the community [who sinned and were forgiven, i.e., the Israelites who worshiped the golden calf].
>
> *And both these instances are necessary; for if [the case of] the individual only were mentioned, [it might have been thought that pardon is granted] because his sin is not generally known. But in the case of a community whose sins are publicly known, it might not be so. And if the case of a community only were mentioned, it might have been thought, because they command greater mercy, but with an individual, whose merits are not so numerous, it is not so; hence both are necessary.*

In this passage, we can clearly see the different layers of the Talmud. The first part of the passage consists of two lovely midrashim on verses from Deuteronomy and Psalms that are woven together to form a unit explaining past communal and individual Israelite misdeeds and the hope they give to repentant sinners. Then, in the paragraph set in italics, the anonymous commentator shows why both cases were necessary.

First, let us explore the context of the Toraitic prooftext used in this passage. The verse from Deuteronomy is placed between the Ten Commandments and the Shema. Interestingly, in this retelling of how the Ten Commandments were given, there is no mention of the golden calf. In this iteration of the moment of revelation, the Israelites are described as completely faithful and bound to receive the reward for their faithfulness. The verse does not exactly fit what we know happened: while Moses was on Mount Sinai, the Israelites made the golden calf. Rabbi Joshua ben Levi explains this apparent contradiction by maintaining that the only reason they built the golden calf was to serve as an example to sinners in future generations that one can always repent no matter how heinous the sin. That's why this verse in Deuteronomy describes the Israelites as faithful of heart: they didn't commit idolatry because they believed in it but merely to give God a chance to demonstrate Divine mercy.

This mention of Israel's idolatry brings up the association with another teaching about the golden calf; this one linking idolatry to adultery. We have the original teaching of Shimon bar Yohai that the Israelites were not idolatrous by nature nor was David adulterous by nature, and he brings prooftexts to prove his points. Both prooftexts feature the word *heart*, whose root לבב *lamed-bet-bet*, seems "doubled" because of the two *bets*. The sages interpret this spelling to refer to a person's inclinations to do evil or good:

> "With all your heart" (Deuteronomy 6:5): With both your inclinations, with the inclination to do good and with the inclination to do evil.
> Another interpretation: "With all your heart (בכל לבבך *b'chol l'vavcha*)": With all that heart that is within you (בכל לב בך *b'chol lev b'cha*); your heart should not be divided in regard to the Omnipresent. [*Sifre D. Piska* 32]

So, in this case in Psalms, David claims that one of his "hearts," his inclination to do evil, is utterly dead within him and he only commits the sin with Bathsheba to open the door for penitents. (For more great interpretations of the story of David and Bathsheba, see *B. Sanhedrin* 107a. And for parallel interpretations of Psalm 109:22, see *B. Berachot* 61b, and *B. Baba Batra* 17a.)

Then the anonymous commentary begins and we can

almost hear the study-session exchange. "Well," one learner
asks, "why did they commit idolatry and adultery?" "It must
be," someone else replies, "to provide examples of repentance
on the individual and communal level, to assure people that you
can recover from sin as an individual person and as a community." (We ought to be careful. This "exchange" is in Hebrew and
thus is likely to be an earlier layer than the portion in italics,
which is in Aramaic and, therefore, probably later.) "O.K., but
why do you need both cases? Wouldn't one example have
sufficed?" "No, because God forgives individuals and communities for different reasons. It's easy for God to forgive an
individual whose sins aren't widely known. Conversely, it's
easy for God to forgive a community because surely, among all
those people, there is enough merit to warrant the forgiveness."
Of course, this explanation assumes that the individual hasn't
sinned in a public way and that there are some decent people in
the community. We could add our own layer of commentary by
asking what happens when the individual's sin is public and the
community is bereft of any merit: does repentance still work?

One of the wonderful things about Judaism is that it does
not demand unrealistic goodness out of us. We are to be as good
as we can be, but we are not angels and God does not respond
to us as angels. Of course, the most famous example of this
precept is the following passage:

> How does Rabbi Yohanan [interpret], "that your brother may
> live with you" (Leviticus 25:36)? He uses it for that which was
> taught: If two are traveling on a road [far from civilization] and
> in the hand of one of them is a pitcher of water, if both drink, they
> will [both] die; if [only] one drinks, he can reach civilization. The
> Son of Patora taught: It is better that both should drink and die,
> rather that one should see his companion's death. Until Rabbi
> Akiba came and taught: "that your brother may live with you":
> your life takes precedence over his life. (B. *Baba Metsia* 62a)

The law follows Rabbi Akiba: we may save our life if we
hold the water. We aren't required to do the saintly thing and
give the water to the other person. The sages were legislating

law, not necessarily mandating the most desirable behavior. It might be the saintly thing to sacrifice your life for someone else's, but the sages knew they could not demand such behavior through law. They could only hold it up as an ideal that some people could attain. This is the difference between the "floor" for behavior that can be legislated and the "ceiling," which can only be encouraged. In general, the sages legislate the minimum required behavior (the "floor") and then encourage a higher standard (the "ceiling").

Our whole long exposition about God's justice and mercy now draws to a close with a *nechemta*, that is, a word of comfort and hope for the future. Notice that the Gemara has scarcely commented on our opening mishnah at all. Rather, it has introduced the themes important to the sages who composed the *Bavli*: the internal state engendered by Israel's monogamous relationship with God that the nations do not have and the consequences that ensue from this basic situation.

> **GEMARA (5b):** Rabbi Yohanan said on behalf of Rabbi Bana'ah: Why is it written, "Happy are you that sow beside all waters, that send forth the feet of the ox and the ass" (Isaiah 32:20)? [It means this:] Happy are you, Israel, when you are occupied with Torah and with acts of kindness. [Then] their [evil] inclination is mastered by them, not they by their inclination, as it is said, "Happy are you that sow beside all waters." And there is no "sowing" except charity (*tsedakah*), as it is said, "Sow to yourselves in righteousness (*litsdakah*), reap according to mercy (*hesed*)" (Hosea 10:12). And there is no "water" except Torah, as it is said, "Oh you who are thirsty come to the water" (Isaiah 55:1). [The phrase] "that send forth the feet of the ox and the ass" [was explained in the] *Tanna debei Eliyahu* thus: A person should always make himself like an ox under a yoke and like an ass carrying burdens concerning [the studying] of words of Torah.

First, let's consider the technical language in this passage. A *tanna* was a repeater of information from a certain school, or house, which in Hebrew is *bayit*, which became shortened to *d'bei*, "of the house of." This phrase, *Tanna d'bei X*, is a pedigree: it tells us who is the originator of this interpretation of Scripture.

This midrash collection, *Tanna debei Eliyahu*, is a collection of teachings from the era of the Mishnah compiled by R. Anan, a Babylonian Amora of the third century C.E.

The verse that is being expounded here is part of a very famous passage from Isaiah, a vision of the bounty which will accompany the flow of God's spirit from on high:

> Then judgment shall dwell in the wilderness and righteousness shall dwell in the fruitful field; and the effect of righteousness, quietness, and assurance forever. And my people shall dwell in a peaceable habitation, and in secure dwellings, and in quiet resting places; and it shall hail in the downfall of the forest that the city shall descend into the valley. Blessed are you that sow beside all waters, that let the feet of the ox and the ass range free. [Isaiah 32:16–20]

This is an image of a land of peace. The cities can descend to the valley because they no longer need be built on hills surrounded by fortified walls. Instead, they can be spread out into valleys where the land is presumably richer. Everyone will have free access to water to make crops plentiful, and there will be an abundance of grazing land for stock. The image of hail falling in the forest is the subject of great debate. It might be a blessing, since the hail can do no substantive damage in the forest.

The other verse from Isaiah is better understood in fuller context:

> Ho, everyone that thirsts, come to the water, and he that has no money come, buy and eat. Come, buy wine and milk without money and without price. Why do you spend money for that which is not bread? And your labor for that which does not satisfy? Hearken diligently to me and eat that which is good and let your soul delight itself in fatness. Incline your ear and come to me: hear, and your soul shall live and I will make an everlasting covenant with you. [Isaiah 55:1–3]

There is an understanding in rabbinic literature that water equals Torah. So, for example, we learn:

And Rabbi Hanina bar Idi said: Why are words of Torah likened unto water, as it is written, "Ho everyone that thirsts, come to the water"? [This is] to say to you: Just as water flows from a higher place to a lower place, so words of Torah are not sustained except in one whose mind is humble. Rabbi Oshaya said: Why are the words of Torah likened unto these three liquids: to water, to wine, and to milk, as it is written, "Ho, everyone that thirsts come for water." And it is written, "Come, buy wine and milk without money and without price"? [This is] to say to you: Just as these three liquids are not sustained except in [the most] humble of vessels, so words of Torah are not sustained except in one whose mind is humble. . . . Another explanation: Just as these three liquids are not spoiled except through inattention, so words of Torah are not forgotten except through inattention. [*B. Taanit* 7a–b]

We also learn (*Sifre* Deuteronomy, *Piska* 48) that Torah is like water because both endure forever, both cleanse the unclean, both restore a person's soul, and both are free to everyone yet both are priceless. (Also see *B. Baba Kamma* 82a and *B. Kiddushin* 30b for more extensions of this metaphor.)

The sages, as they often do, spiritualize the concrete, physical aspects of Torah. (Remember that we saw, above, their proclivity for concretizing and quantifying the spiritual aspects of Judaism. This is the counterbalance to that tendency.) How do they reinterpret Isaiah's scenario? It's not about farming and herding; this passage is referring to good deeds and Torah, according to the sages. The opportunity to farm is reinterpreted as doing good deeds, which is similar to agriculture: One does the deed and only later reaps the reward.

The metaphors for Torah brought forward here are classic: Torah is like a tree and like water. Water sustains life and trees sustain life, and land, as well. This passage promises a time of peace and plenty when every faithful Jew will be rewarded. However, even in this utopian vision, the sages are honest with us: Torah study is hard work and requires diligence. Just as wells must be dug, water drawn from them, and cisterns filled with them, so Torah study requires labor. The Jewish ideal is not one of ease. Life, and life hereafter, is not about having fun. It's about having meaning, and meaning can only be acquired through diligence in good deeds and Torah study.

### Practical Advice on Living in a Non-Jewish World

Now that the Gemara has introduced, at length, the core of its interpretation of this tractate, it finally returns to the topic the Mishnah introduced regarding economic exchanges with idolaters at particularly idolatrous times. The person encountered is here described as a *min*, a Judeo-Christian. (We use the term here not as it is popularly used today but to refer to Jews who converted to Christianity.) The word *min* can also refer to Gnostics and Sadducees. There is obviously some blurring of the categories in the Gemara between the categories idolater and *min*. (An old, though still valuable, resource for exploring the identity of the *min* is Herford's *Christianity in Talmud and Midrash*.)

> **GEMARA (6b):** A certain *min* once sent on his festival day a Casearean denar to Rabbi Yehudah Nesia while Reish Lakish was sitting before him. Said he, "What shall I do? If I accept it, he will go and praise [the idols for it]. If I do not accept it, he will be displeased." Reish Lakish said to him, "Take it and drop it into a well in his presence." He [Yehudah Nesia said], "This will displease him all the more!" "I mean you should do it by sleight of hand."

Here we have a case involving a situation covered by our mishnah: a sage is offered a coin on a pagan festival. This money, coined in commemoration of the Caesar's coronation or at Caesarea in Cappadocia, the only colony that enjoyed the right of coinage in gold under the Romans, was problematic because it had some sort of image on it. Either the coin had the king's likeness or the image of a pagan god. So we have an idolatrous person offering an idolatrous object to a Jew on an idolatrous day. Rabbi Yehudah is stymied as to what to do, and Reish Lakish, who before he became a sage was a gladiator and was thus quite familiar with the Roman world, suggests a tactful solution: he should drop it "accidentally" in sight of the messenger. Then, the messenger would know the coin was not accepted but that there is a plausible reason for the rejection. The Jewish solution to this delicate situation does not require heroics. Instead, there is a balance between ideology and the need to get along with others.

Similar situations constantly confront Jews today. Although Christmas is not a pagan holiday, it is still a time when our surrounding culture makes us aware that we are in the minority. How do we react when we receive Christmas cards and presents or when the clerk in the store says "Merry Christmas" while handing us the receipt? In intermarried families these issues can become particularly thorny. This story seems to convey that we should be clear about who we are without offending others who are celebrating their own holidays. In family situations, it might be best to clearly communicate the rules about holiday gifts at the outset of relationships. One can use birthdays as an analogy. We send people presents on their birthdays, not on our own. Therefore, it follows that we send Christmas cards and gifts to Christians for their holiday, and Christians should send us Hannukkah gifts and cards. Anything else would be impolite and theologically incorrect.

Of course, there are Jews who, even though not intermarried, have Christmas trees in their homes, have no mezuzahs on their doors, and do not say the Shema each day. Such Jews have ancient ancestors in a group called *amei ha'arets*, literally "the people of the land," a phrase that denotes a group with lax observance of Judaism. An *am ha'arets* is the opposite of a *chaveir*, literally "a friend," that is, one who takes great care to observe all the rules of Judaism as the sages demanded, particularly with regard to Jewish agricultural taxes (e.g., tithes) and ritual purity. There is a great deal of discussion in rabbinic literature about what sort of behavior includes or excludes one from membership in this group. In our next passage, which is the last of the Gemara's discussion of this first mishnah, and a *nechemta*, the overwhelming power of repentance is stressed.

GEMARA (7a): Our Rabbis taught: If they [*amei ha'arets* who had become *chaveirim*] reverted [to their usual practices] none of them should ever be accepted [i.e., regarded as *chaveirim* again]. These are the words of Rabbi Meir. Rabbi Yehudah says: If they reverted in secret matters, we do not accept them. [If] in public [matters], we accept them. Some say: If they [reverted to their misdeeds] in private, we accept them. (7b) [If they reverted in public] we do not accept them. Rabbi Shimon and Rabbi Yehoshua ben Karcha says: Whether in the one case or in the other we should accept them, for it is said, "Return, o backsliding children" (Jeremiah 3:14). Said Rabbi Yitschak, a man of Kefar Acco, in the name of Rabbi Yohanan: The halakhah is according to this [latter] pair.

We might be somewhat puzzled by this discussion. Our mishnah talks about idolaters, and here we speak of Jews, albeit nonobservant ones. At least two explanations suggest themselves. On the one hand, there are some who believe that *amei ha'arets* were the Jewish seedbed from which Christianity sprung, and this could constitute the thematic link between this material and our mishnah (Oppenheimer 1977, 218–299). On the other hand, the sages may be observing here something that modern sociologists have noted: the borders of the Jewish community are fluid and permeable. It is not really a clear-cut, black-and-white matter: you are a Jew or you are not. Rather, the matter could better be described as a range with "Least Jewish" at one end and "Most Jewish" on the other and a distribution of Jews along that range. An *am ha'arets* would be at the "Least Jewish" extreme, while a *chaveir* would be at the "Most Jewish" end. People probably slid along this scale then as Jews do now, and that is what is at issue in this passage.

Was there ever a person who fell off the scale because of lax observance of Judaism? Rabbi Meir thinks so: according to him, *amei ha'arets* who tried to be observant but then slipped back to their old ways could never be readmitted into the company of those who kept Judaism strictly. Then we have other opinions. Some say, if the *amei ha'arets* violated Judaism privately, they can be welcomed back, while others disagree with this. Yet others say that whether their transgression was public or private, their repentance is always efficacious.

My student Elizabeth Weinberg developed Table 1–1 to enumerate the opinions listed in this passage.

**Table 1–1.**

| Can This Jew Be Taken Back? | | |
|---|---|---|
| | Public Transgression | Private Transgression |
| Rabbi Meir | No | No |
| Rabbi Yehudah | Yes | No |
| "Some say" | No | Yes |
| R. Shimon & R. Yehoshua | Yes | Yes |
| Rabbi Yitshak | Yes | Yes |

This passage is clearly composed to present the most exclusive view first, intermediate views second, and the most inclusive view last, ending with the definitive statement that the most inclusive view is the law. The point of this composition seems to underscore the importance of leaving the door open to Jews who wish to return.

An example may help clarify this. There is a difference between a Jew wearing a cross in public and a Jew having a cross at home. Both are violations of Judaism, but one involves the honor of the community and one does not. How easy would it be to accept back at synagogue a Jew who had previously come to services wearing a big cross and driving a car with a bumper sticker that said "Jesus Loves Me?" Would it be harder to accept this person back into the community than one who just wore a cross at home? No matter how difficult, the law is that we accept all Jews back when they repent.

Another example may help. In the Orthodox community there are "BTs," that is, *Ba'alei Teshuvah*, persons who were not raised as observant Jews and who have become observers of the rules of *kashrut*, family purity, and Shabbat. Then there are the "FFBs," those "Frum from birth" who came from observant homes. The FFBs accept the BTs into their communities and synagogues, even when these people may have previously dined on pork, had Christmas trees, and eaten on Yom Kippur.

One is allowed to slide along the scale toward greater Jewishness with relatively little communal penalty for past lapses in Jewish observance. The sages wanted to facilitate any tendency in this direction and so mandated an accepting attitude toward Jews who, in the past, may have ignored their Judaism.

We at last move on to our second mishnah, which is really a clarification of our first. The first mishnah of the tractate forbid Jews to do business with idolaters for three days before their festivals. This mishnah explores that theme in a bit more detail.

> **MISHNAH (7b):** Rabbi Yishmael says: [On the] three [days] before their [festivals] and [on the] three [days] after [their festivals] it [commerce] is forbidden. And the sages say, before their festivals it [commerce] is prohibited [but] afterward it is permitted.

> **GEMARA:** Said Rav Tahlifa bar Avdimi in the name of Shmuel: According to Rabbi Yishmael it should always be forbidden [to transact business with idolaters because of] Sunday. . . . Shmuel said: In the Diaspora the prohibition is limited to their festival days [only].

Let us examine our mishnah first and then what the Gemara makes of it. An individual opinion is expressed that we should refrain from all the activities mentioned in our first mishnah (e.g., lending idolaters items, repaying debts to them, etc.) not only on the three days before their holiday but for three days after it, as well. This view is rejected by the majority, who hold with the original ruling of the mishnah: for three days before the holiday these transactions are forbidden but they are permitted after the holiday is over.

The Gemara comments that it would never be possible to transact business with non-Jews according to Rabbi Yishmael because Sunday has three days preceding it and three following it. Perhaps this was Rabbi Yishmael's intention: to prohibit all transactions with idolaters. Is Rabbi Yishmael referring to an idolatrous weekly worship day on Sundays or is he referring to Christian worship on Sundays? It is difficult to know. One of the problems with this tractate, and with passages that deal with idolaters and *minim* in general, is that they were subject to censorship through the centuries. This has led to many textual discrepancies in the Talmud as we now have it.

The Mishnah was composed in the Land of Israel, while this Gemara was composed in Babylonia. Being out of the Land changed the way the sages thought about this problem. A comparison with today's world may help clarify this change. In the State of Israel today, it is possible to almost completely avoid doing business with non-Jews if one so desires. One can choose to live in an exclusively Jewish neighborhood and only buy from merchants there. The stores that sell Jewish ritual items in Jerusalem's *Meiah She'arim*, an extremely observant neighborhood, for example, probably do very little business with non-Jews. However, in the United States most business people would go bankrupt if they tried to sell only to Jews. Indeed, it would substantially hurt most stores' sales to forgo selling to non-Jews for the three days before Christmas. Shmuel understands this dynamic and rules that outside the Land of Israel, merchants are forbidden to sell to idolaters only on the day of the holiday itself, perhaps recognizing how dependent Jewish merchants in Babylonia were on non-Jews for their economic survival.

There *is* a difference between Jewish life in the Land/State of Israel and outside of it. We are more dependent on the non-Jewish community for economic, political, and military survival than are Jews in Israel. There is a price to be paid for this dependence, and that is a requirement that we work with non-Jews and live, at least partly, in a non-Jewish world. If that price seems too high, we have the luxury of being able to easily make *aliyah* and go to Israel. This move, from the non-Jewish world to a Jewish one, can be made in miniature, individual, incremental steps. It happens every time we opt for a Jewish camp over a non-Jewish one or a Jewish day-school over a non-Jewish one. Each such step makes one's ties to secular culture weaker in favor of a stronger Jewish identity, and each Jew must make the journey through these decisions for himself or herself.

### Martyrdom and Torah

Part of the Jewish experience of the idolatrous world in the rabbinic era was the persecution and martyrdom of Jews.

Another, more inspiring part of that experience was the "righteous gentiles" of that age who would not harm Jews even when ordered to do so by the highest authorities. The following is the story of one such righteous gentile. Indeed, this is part of a long passage about righteous gentiles and non-Jews who become Jews. The Gemara, again separating from the Mishnah's agenda, is further exploring the concept that God is forgiving, accepts with grace the righteous deeds of non-Jews, and welcomes converts to Judaism. This balances the hostile attitude toward non-Jews that we saw before, exposing the real, inward truth: it is not non-Jews that the sages detest but rather the idolatry within them that is the target of their ire.

Just as the sages hated the idolatry pagans practiced, they could express great reverence for non-Jews who understood the meaning of monotheism. A fine example is someone they call Keti'ah bar Shalom, which means, "the circumcised one, son of peace" or "through circumcision he has peace." He was probably Flavius Clemens, Domitian's nephew, who was executed for Judaising toward the end of Domitian's reign (c. 96 c.e.).

> **GEMARA (10b):** There was once a Caesar who hated the Jews. He said to the important [persons] of the government: "If one has a wart on his foot, shall he cut it away and live [in comfort] or leave it on and suffer discomfort?" They said: "He should cut it away and live [in comfort]." Keti'ah bar Shalom said to them: "In the first place, you cannot do away with all of them, for it is written, 'For I have spread you abroad as the four winds of the heaven' (Zecharia 2:10). What does this verse mean? Were it to mean that [Israel] was to be scattered *by* the four corners of the world, then instead of saying *as* the four winds, the verse would have said *by* the four winds? Rather, [it can only mean that] just as the world cannot exist without winds, so the world cannot exist without Israel. And what is more, your kingdom will be called a crippled (*k'ti'ah*) kingdom." He [the Caesar] said to him: "You have spoken well, [however] he who contradicts the king is to be cast into a furnace." On his being led away, a matron said of him: "Pity the ship that sails [toward the harbor] without paying the tax." Then, throwing himself on his foreskin he cut it away (*k'ta'ah*) and said: "You have paid the tax you will pass and enter [paradise].". . . A *Bat Kol* exclaimed [as he died]: "Keti'ah

bar Shalom is destined for [eternal] life in the world to come!"
Rabbi [on hearing of it] wept and said: "There are those who
acquire their eternity in one hour and there are those who acquire
their eternity [over] many years!"

It seems that there may have been a Roman of high rank
who was sympathetic to Judaism and may have converted
before his death. For this, the sages praise him. The symmetry in
the story is clear. The evil Caesar wants to cut away the Jews
from life, an evil act. Keti'ah bar Shalom cuts away his foreskin
and achieves life eternal. Their actions and motivations are the
opposite of each other.

The term *Bat Kol* can mean a Heavenly Voice, it can denote
public opinion or, as may happen, both at the same time. One of
the most appealing aspects of Judaism is its democratic nature.
God is presumed to speak through the public opinion of
average, faithful Jews. For example, when Hillel came from
Babylonia to the Land of Israel, he could not remember a certain
law relating to the Passover offering and looked to lay people for
the answer:

I have heard this halakhah but have forgotten it: but leave [it]
to Israel, if they are not prophets they are the sons of prophets. [*B.
Pesachim* 66b]

Holiness and wisdom do not reside only with sages and
rabbis in Judaism, and any rabbis who forget this do so at their
peril. In the case of Keti'ah ben Shalom, one man's piety inspires
one of the greatest sage's admiration. Rabbi Yehudah Hanasi
labored to live his whole life piously in order to achieve
redemption while Keti'ah ben Shalom attains it in one act of
martyrdom.

Rabbi's comment highlights the power of conversion experiences. It is true that those who are born Jewish and have
learned Judaism their whole lives have an ease and a natural-
ness about their observance that is enviable. It is also true that
those who come to Judaism from non-Jewish backgrounds and
those who were born Jewish but abandoned that Judaism and
then returned to it often have an intensity about their Jewishness

that is enviable as well. That, perhaps, is the essence of the *Bat Kol*, God's voice as expressed through Jewish public opinion, as it is heard in Keti'ah ben Shalom's story. We can easily imagine a Jewish crowd proclaiming Keti'ah ben Shalom's redemption as he is being led away to execution. Thus, the two sorts of Judaism, the one that flows from the generations and the one that arises suddenly from outside that stream, acclaim one another. Keti'ah ben Shalom observes circumcision, the symbol of the continuity of the generations, while the Jewish community accepts and is inspired by his faithfulness.

The Gemara now brings another example of how Judaism can be enriched by converts, in this case, a man named Onkelos. To Onkelos, who is often confused with Aquila in our sources, is attributed a translation of the Bible into Aramaic. His translation can be found in Jewish versions of Scripture (called *Mikra'ot Gedolot*) to this day. Onkelos lived in the second century c.e. and was said to observe the mitzvot with great care. Apparently the Emperor Hadrian opposed his conversion, as is recorded in the following legend.

> **GEMARA (11a):** [When] Onkelos bar Kalonymus became a proselyte, the Caesar sent a contingent of Roman [soldiers] after him [to arrest him], but he enticed them by [citing] Scripture and they became converted [to Judaism].
>
> [The Caesar] sent another Roman contingent [of soldiers] [and] he said to them, "Don't say anything to him." As they were taking him away, he said to them, "Let me say an ordinary thing to you: [In a procession] the torchlighter carries the light in front of the torchbearer, the torchbearer in front of the leader, the leader in front of the governor, the governor in front of the chief officer; but does the chief officer carry the light in front of the people [that follow]?" They said to him, "No." Said he to them: "[Yet] the Holy One, blessed be He, does carry the light before Israel, as it is written, 'And the Lord went before them . . . in a pillar of fire to give them light'" (Exodus 13:21). Then they all became converted.
>
> Again he [the Caesar] sent another contingent. He said to them: "Don't have any conversation whatever with him." So they took hold of him; and as they were walking on he saw the mezuzah that was fixed on the door-frame. He put his hand on it

and said to them, "What is this?" They said to him, "Tell us." Said he, "According to the custom of the world, a king of flesh and blood dwells within, and his servants keep guard on him without; while [in the case of] the Holy One, blessed be He, it is His servants who dwell within while He keeps guard on them from without; as it is said: "The Lord shall guard your going out and your coming in from this time forth and for evermore" (Psalm 121:8).

Perhaps some representatives of the emperor visited Onkelos, and he shared with them some Scriptures and converted them. It might also be that the two specific examples are later persons' ideas of what might have taken place in that interchange and then the story may have been framed in a classic, tripartite sequence, making them separate incidents.

The latter two incidents are obviously designed to contrast the emperor's rule with God's kingship. Interestingly, both of Onkelos' examples focus on how God cares for the Jews communally and individually as contrasted with an earthly king who is cared for by other human beings. In other words, he is asking those serving the emperor, "Would you rather serve a human king or be served by a Divine one?" When framed in this way, only a fool would decide that Judaism did not offer the better deal. Interestingly, Onkelos chooses as the selling points for Judaism its nonhierarchical nature and God's nurturing character combined with God's obvious royal power. Onkelos highlights the very heart of Judaism—*power within, and bound by, relationship*—as its best attribute.

Who is the best person to "sell" Judaism to others? First of all, we might think that Judaism doesn't need to be "sold": it is attractive in and of itself once one enters its sphere, drawing people toward its center as a star draws planets into its orbit. Perhaps we might better ask, "Who is best to draw people into Judaism's sphere of influence?" If we are to believe our texts, those who have converted to Judaism or those who have returned to it (*ba'alei teshuvah*) are our best representatives. Why? Perhaps because they have a familiarity with, and therefore understanding of, both spheres: the non-Jewish world and the world of Judaism. Through their excitement about the Judaism they are discovering, such persons can inspire others.

They are also inspiring in that they show that it can be done. A person can go from knowing no Hebrew and nothing about Jewish traditions to being able, like Onkelos, to translate Hebrew Scriptures in a way that lasts for two thousand years. There is a lot to learn in Judaism, but anyone can do it no matter how late they start.

Judaism takes a balanced view of life. On the one hand, we focus on the spiritual, on the inner essence of our deeds as religious expression. On the other hand, appearances and physical acts are important, as well. There is also, as we have already seen, a balance between theological desiderata and minimum Jewish legal standards. All these "balancing acts" are evident in the following passage.

> **GEMARA (12a):** If a splinter has got into his [foot] while in front of an idol, he should not bend down to get it out, because he may appear to be bowing to the idol; but if it does not appear [that he is bowing to an idol], it is permitted. If his coins were scattered in front of an idol he should not bend and pick them up, for it may appear that he was bowing to the idol; but if it will not appear [that way], it is permitted. If there is a spring flowing in front of an idol, he should not bend down and drink, because it may appear that he is bowing to the idol; but if it does not appear [that he is bowing to the idol], it is permitted.

Whether we like it or not, appearances are important. We must take care, the sages contend in this passage, not to appear to bow before an idol. On the other hand, they realize that it would be hard for persons with splinters in their feet to keep walking or for persons who had dropped their money to keep from picking it up. Therefore, what they seem to be mandating in this passage is prevention and cure at the same time. First, be careful not to get into situations that might make it appear that you are bowing before an idol. However, if you do get into such a situation, be sure to make it evident by your manner that you are not bowing before the idol but taking a splinter out of your foot, picking up coins, or getting a drink of water.

It is difficult for Americans to imagine this problem. We are a society largely devoid of statues that could have been made as idols. However, one visit to Europe could make clear how ubiquitous this phenomenon was. In Europe there are ancient statues of gods everywhere, and the scenario outlined in the Gemara really could occur. An American analogy, inexact though it might be, would be a Jew's presence in church. Imagine you are attending the wedding of Catholic friends. You wouldn't want to kneel during the Mass or make the sign of the cross. You would refrain from kneeling not only out of respect for Judaism, but out of respect for Catholicism. To kneel without understanding or partaking in the meaning of the ritual would be to make a mockery of your friend's faith. However, if your pearl necklace broke and you had to get down on your hands and knees to collect the pearls before people tripped and fell on them, the sages would permit you to do so as long as you make it clear that you are collecting your pearls rather than kneeling at the cross.

Our next mishnah deals with this same issue of appearances. It may bring to mind parallels with our own lives. Each December we are inundated with Christmas decorations in stores and Christmas music on the radio. This can cause a good bit of dissonance since it seems that everyone is celebrating a holiday that we do not share. The sages also experienced this sort of dissonance during idolatrous festival seasons.

> **MISHNAH (12b):** A city in which idolatry is taking place, some of its shops being decorated with garlands and some not decorated—this was the case of Beit Shean—and the sages said: in the decorated ones it is forbidden [to buy], but in the undecorated ones it is permitted.

What is going on here? Let us say that a city is preparing for an idolatrous festival in Israel but it is still not three days before the holiday. Therefore, Jews are permitted to do business in this city. However, the shops that had holiday decorations were signifying that part of their proceeds were dedicated to idolatry, much as today merchants advertise that five percent of each sale is donated to some cause. The sages rule that one may not purchase goods in those shops in which idolatry would be supported from the proceeds.

Now, what should today's Jews do in terms of making purchases in stores with Christmas decorations that have no significance other than seasonal marketing? (We will leave undiscussed the way this commercialization of a holiday makes pious Christians feel.) Should you buy in such stores? Do you let your child sit in Santa's lap? Where do you draw your line? The sages are suggesting two criteria to help you decide: do your activities give the appearance of adhering to another religion and what eventually happens to the money you spend?

Perhaps more extreme examples make the issue clearer. What if we went into a store and learned that a part of every purchase would go to support the KKK or a neo-Nazi group? What if part of every purchase went to an organization that tried to convert Jews to Christianity? Our mishnah suggests that we should not make purchases in such stores.

While the sages loved the figures of Keti'ah ben Shalom and Onkelos, they were far more familiar with oppression of Jews by non-Jews as exemplified by Hadrian. This Roman emperor ruled from 117–138 C.E. and was not, at first, hostile to Jews. He crushed the Bar Kohba Revolt (132–135 C.E.), built a gentile city called Aelia Capitolina on the site where Jerusalem had stood, and issued harsh decrees against the study of Torah and the practice of Judaism. Those who refused to obey these edicts were martyred, among them, Rabbi Akiba and Rabbi Hanina ben Teradion. It is the latter's story that is preserved, with many embellishments, in our tractate.

**GEMARA (17b):** They then brought up Rabbi Hanina ben Teradion and they said to him: Why have you occupied yourself with Torah (forbidden by Hadrian under penalty of death)? He said to them: Thus the Lord my God commanded me. At once they sentenced him to be burnt, his wife to be slain, and his daughter to be consigned to a brothel.

([The punishment of being] burnt came upon him because he [18a] pronounced the Name in its full spelling. But how could he do so? Have we not learned: These are they who have no portion in the world to come: He who says the Torah is not from Heaven or that the resurrection of the dead is not taught in the Torah. Abba Shaul says: Also he who pronounces the Name in its full spelling [*Sanhedrin*, Mishnah 10:1, *Bavli* 90a]? . . . His wife was punished by being slain, because she did not prevent him [from saying the Name this way in public]. From this it was deduced: Anyone who has the power to prevent [one from doing wrong] and does not prevent [the sin], is punished for him [B. *Shabbat* 54b]. His daughter was consigned to a brothel, for Rabbi Yohanan related that once his daughter was walking in front of some great men of Rome who said, "How beautiful are the steps of this maiden!" Immediately, she took particular care of her steps, which confirms what Rabbi Shimon ben Lakish said: What is the meaning of the verse, "The iniquity of my heel compasses me about" [Psalm 49:6]?—Sins that one treads under heel in this world compass him about on the Day of Judgment.)

As the three of them went out [from the tribunal] they accepted the righteousness of [the Divine] righteous judgment. He quoted: "The Rock, His work is perfect; [for all His ways are justice]" (Deuteronomy 32:4). And his wife said [the second part of the verse]: "A God of faithfulness and without iniquity, just and right is He" (Deuteronomy 32:4). His daughter said: "Great in counsel and mighty in work, whose eyes are open upon all the ways [of the sons of men, to give everyone according to his ways, and according to the fruit of his doing]" (Jeremiah 32:19). Said Rabbi: How great were these righteous ones, that three scriptural passages, [expressing] acceptance of [Divine] righteous justice, readily occurred to them, just at the [appropriate] time for accepting the righteousness of [Divine] judgment. . . .

Rabbi Hanina ben Teradion was sitting and occupying himself with the Torah, publicly gathering assemblies, and keeping a Scroll of the Law in his bosom. Straight away they took hold of him, wrapped him in the Scroll of the Law, placed bundles of branches round him, and set them on fire. They then brought tufts of wool, which they had soaked in water, and placed them over his heart, so that his soul should not leave quickly. His daughter said to him, "Father, that I should see you in this state!" He said to her, "If it were I alone being burnt it would have been a thing hard for me [to bear; but] now that I am burning together with the Scroll of the Law, He who will have regard for the plight of the Torah will also have regard for my plight." His students said to him, "Rabbi, what do you see?" He said to them, "The parchments are being burnt but the letters are flying [free]."

"Open then your mouth so that the fire enter into you." He said to them, "Better that the One who gave me [my soul should be the One to] take it away, but no one should injure himself." The executioner said to him: Rabbi, if I raise the flame and take away the tufts of wool from over your heart, will you cause me to enter into the life to come? He said to him: Yes. He [the executioner] said to him: Then swear unto me. He swore unto him. He immediately raised the flame and removed the tufts of wool from over his heart, and his soul quickly departed. The executioner then jumped and threw himself into the fire. And a *Bat Kol* went forth [saying]: Rabbi Hanina ben Teradion and the executioner are destined for life in the World to Come. [When] Rabbi [heard it] he wept and said: "There are those who acquire their eternity in one hour and there are those who acquire their eternity [over] many years!"

Rabbi Hanina's story contains three basic themes that we will examine in turn. (1) What is the most sinless sin? (2) What is the appropriate response to tragedy? (3) How should one face death?

The part of this passage that describes why Rabbi Hanina and his family merited death is obviously a later addition to our text. For earlier generations, the execution of Rabbi Hanina, Rabbi Akiba, and the other martyrs was a searing wound on the body of the Jewish people. There was no attempt to suggest that the martyrs had actually deserved their fate. There was straightforward anguish and anger at God expressed through the question, "This is Torah and this is its reward?!?" (*B. Berachot* 61b, *B. Menachot* 29b and *Y. Hagigah* 2:1, 77b). After the Bar Kokhba Revolt and the Hadrianic persecutions, there was obviously a tremendous feeling of disappointment in God. How could God let the most righteous teachers in Israel suffer such horrible deaths? This is like the outrage we feel after being robbed (and, indeed, the Jewish people were robbed of some of their greatest leaders). We are scared. We are mad. We don't want it to have happened, and we want things back the way they were before. Only later do we start to think, "What could I have done differently to avoid this?" Only this second phase of response to tragedy is found in this passage as well as a third, acceptance.

In later generations, Jews must have struggled to keep their concept of a just God intact while knowing that these horrible executions took place. So they imagined what the most sinless sin that could merit the death penalty would be and attributed that to Rabbi Hanina. They determined that the most "pure" sin was speaking God's true name. As those who struggle to learn Hebrew discover to their chagrin, God's name, spelled with the letters *yud-hey-vav-hey*, is pronounced in a completely different way in order not to say God's actual name. God's actual name was only to be pronounced in the most holy of environments: the innermost chamber of the Temple. Rabbi Hanina's wife was apparently consigned to death because she did not stop him from uttering this name, and his daughter, for a small act of immodesty, was sent to a brothel. Though the punishments may seem incredibly harsh, there is at least some correlation between sin and punishment. Some attempt is made to make sense of God's permitting these executions to happen. After all, one of the biggest, if not *the* biggest, difference between Judaism and idolatry is the covenantal nature of the Jewish people's relationship with God. God is predictable. Idolatrous gods were capricious. The innovation of Judaism was the idea that if we were faithful, then God was bound to be faithful. To keep these executions from appearing to be God's capricious whim or, worse, that God did not care, some sin had to be found in those executed. But the sin had to be the least noxious that could still merit punishment.

Rabbi Hanina, his wife, and his daughter all respond to their punishment with perfect acceptance. They are beyond the phase of outrage and even beyond the phase of trying to determine their own role in causing this moment. They express their acceptance of their fate by reciting verses of praise to God. They can see the justice in this moment even if those looking on cannot. As Rava notes of this story, it takes great composure to recall the perfectly appropriate line of Scripture at such a moment. He marvels at their poise that expresses true quietude of the soul. Did they actually say these things or were these statements attributed to them later on? Does it matter? What became important for later generations was the ability to accept martyrdom with perfect faith, and this is what is highlighted in the story. God's faithfulness, even though difficult to understand, is answered by utter human faithfulness. This is the core of Judaism that no earthly power can destroy.

The story of Rabbi Hanina's execution is one of the most heart-rending in all of rabbinic literature. The tufts of wet wool were placed over the condemned man's heart in order to cool it and allow it to continue beating for as long as possible so that the torture of immolation would linger. Rabbi Hanina's statement about the scrolls burning and the letters soaring is a metaphor for every dying: the body is destroyed and the soul is liberated. He experiences death without trying to hold on to life.

Few of us can face the actual process of dying without ambivalence, without feeling pulled toward uncompleted business here on earth. At the moment of death many of us would probably be absorbed in looking back and holding on rather than experiencing the passage from life to death itself to the fullest. The goal is to live one's life in such a way that death could be experienced unambivalently. That is, one should strive to live a life that will yield no regrets, but rather a feeling of peace. This, manifestly, was what Rabbi Hanina experienced.

Rabbi Yehudah Hanasi reacts in the same way that he did when hearing of Keti'ah ben Shalom and his bravery. He is wistfully appreciative of these dramatic acts that were a result of tumultuous times. While they are tremendously appealing and inspiring, they are not the stuff of average lives. Very few of us would choose to earn our redemption in this way. Judaism is a religion of life that glorifies heroic death only when that death is unavoidable. How blessed we are that our religion does not require such exceptional acts to earn redemption! Merely by living a life of Torah and mitzvot day by day we can be the equals of Rabbi Hanina, the executioner and Keti'ah ben Shalom.

## How to Study Torah

This concept, that a simple life lived in the light of Torah is heroic, leads the sages to an extended discussion of how one should correctly study Torah and live according to it. One passage in this discussion illustrates the true, but often overlooked, point that we don't usually become sinners or saints all of a sudden, but step by tiny step.

> **GEMARA (18b):** Rabbi Shimon ben Pazi expounded [the foregoing verse as follows]: What does Scripture mean by, "Happy is the man that has not walked in the counsel of the wicked, nor stood in the way of sinners, nor sat in the seat of the scornful" (Psalm 1:1). If he did not walk [that way] at all, how could he stand there? And if he did not stand there, he obviously did not sit [among them], and as he did not sit among them, he could not have scorned! The wording is to teach you that if one walks [towards the wicked], in the end he will stand with them, and if he stands in the end, he will sit with them, and if he does sit, in the end he will come to scorn, and if he does scorn, the scriptural verse will be applicable to him, "If you are wise for yourself, and if you scorn, you alone shall bear it" (Proverbs 9:12).

Rabbi Shimon ben Pazi is expounding the first psalm, which graphically portrays the difference between a Torah-loving, wise person and a wicked one who despises Torah:

> Happy is the man that has not walked in the counsel of the wicked, nor stood in the way of sinners, nor sat in the seat of the scornful. But his delight is in the law of the Lord, and in His law does he meditate day and night. And he shall be like a tree planted by streams of water that brings forth its fruit in its season and whose leaf does not wither; and in whatsoever he does he shall prosper.
> Not so the wicked; but they are like the chaff, which the wind drives away. Therefore the wicked shall not stand in the judgment, nor sinners in the congregation of the righteous. For the Lord regards the way of the righteous, but the wicked shall perish. [Psalm 1]

This is a perfect psalm for the sages to elaborate on since it so aptly expresses their viewpoint: it advocates righteousness through Torah and justice for the wicked. In his charming exposition, Rabbi Shimon ben Pazi shows how the most casual contact with a sinner can lead a righteous person into more and more such contact that will eventually cause that person's downfall. But, he asserts, if one avoids such contact from the very first opportunity, when it is relatively more easy to turn away, then one has a greater chance of avoiding it altogether. This truth is encapsulated in Mishnah *Pirkei Avot* 4:2: "One mitzvah begets another and one sin begets another." So the study of Torah, and living a life of mitzvot, needs communal support. It is hard to keep kosher or Shabbat when no one around you is supporting you and doing the same. It is easier to do these mitzvot in a milieu in which others are observing them.

The sages know that learning must take into account the nature and talents of the individual. They allow this individual freedom in the pursuit of Torah:

> GEMARA (19a): "But whose desire is in the law of the Lord" (Psalm 1:2). Said Rabbi: A person can learn only that part of the Torah that is his heart's desire, for it is said, "But whose *desire* is in the law of the Lord."

Rabbi is here saying that you can only learn what you're meant to learn, what it is your soul's destiny to learn. God gives to each person a task in life and the talents to do that task. Those who are destined to do scientific research might try to become physicians and might even be rather good at medicine. But they would never have the feeling of soaring, of floating, of peace that they would achieve were they to study the thing they were meant to study.

When we are doing what God intends for us to do, then we are achieving Torah in our lives, even if it is not the explicit study of a Jewish text. How? Because when we then subsequently study a Jewish text, we can relate the text to what is happening in our lives and the text's truth becomes clear to us. A saying from the Talmud about peace won't mean much to a person who experiences no inner peace, who has no real spiritual referent for the term. Only when we flow with the direction God desires for our lives can we begin to really understand, for example, the story of Rabbi Hanina's acceptance of his fate.

Torah, whether in life experience or straight textual form, is not something that can be acquired once, like a vaccine of enlightenment, and then kept up with booster shots every ten years or so. This next passage reflects that Torah must be acquired gradually and consistently.

> GEMARA (19a): Said Rava in the name of Rav Sehorah, who said it in the name of Rav Huna (*B. Eruvin* 54b): What is the meaning of the verse, "Wealth gotten by vanity shall be diminished, but he that gathers little by little shall increase" (Proverbs 13:11)?—If one studies by heaps at a time, he will benefit but little, but if one gathers [knowledge] little by little, he will gain much.

This passage calls to mind students who study intensely for their Bar or Bat Mitzvah and then quit religious school the day after the ceremony. Such learning has some merit, but it does not last. No wonder these people think Judaism is such an unsatisfying religion: they never came to an adult appreciation of it! They stopped studying it when they were adolescents and so their view of Judaism is frozen at this stage. Imagine how good a scientist would be if she stopped studying science in seventh grade or how good a writer would be if he quit English classes in eighth grade. So it should not be surprising when a Jew cannot function competently, having stopped studying Judaism at puberty. (Incidentally, this passage in *B. Eruvin* is another lovely section of text on how one learns effectively.)

So how does a person learn? The Gemara suggests that we learn best by exposing ourselves to several teachers rather than confining ourselves to one approach.

> GEMARA (19a): "And he shall be like a tree transplanted by streams of water" (Psalm 1:3). Those of the school of Rabbi Yannai said: "a tree *transplanted*," not "a tree *planted*"—[which implies that] whoever learns Torah from one master only will never see a sign of blessing. Said Rav Hisda to the rabbinic students: I have a mind to tell you something, though I fear that you might leave me and go elsewhere: Whoever learns Torah from one master only will never see a sign of blessing [i.e., achieve success]. They did leave him and went [to sit] before Rabbah. He said to them: these words [apply only to lessons in] logical deduction (*svara*), but as to oral traditions (*gemara*) it is

better to learn from one master only, so that (19b) one is not to be confused by the variation in terms used.

This exposition is trying to explain why the psalm uses the verb *shatul*, transplanted, instead of the more common verb, *nata'*, planted, to describe the tree that is a metaphor for a scholar. The suggestion is that one should learn from many different teachers rather than just one. Even the greatest teacher has limitations and can only teach so much. If one becomes a disciple of one teacher and never learns from many, then one cannot develop one's own voice and become a genuine teacher in one's own turn.

A distinction between *svara* and *gemara* is drawn in this passage. These are two broad categories of knowledge in rabbinic literature. *Svara* is a logical deduction that can be used to generate Jewish law. *Gemara* is a tradition handed down from teacher to pupil. We can think of the difference between *gemara* and *svara* as the difference between exact recipes and cooking skills. One must be followed to the letter; the other can be used to generate new recipes. Naturally, both sorts of learning are useful and create a tension within Jewish intellectual life between what is received from previous generations and what can be created in each generation. As always, balance is the key.

According to David Goodblatt (1975) the major difference between study in Israel and in Babylonia was that in Israel it was accomplished in institutions and in Babylonia it was more often done in small, personalized teaching circles:

By "school" I mean an institution which transcends its principals. It has a staff, a curriculum, and, most important, a life of its own, a corporate identity. Students come and go, teachers leave and are replaced, the head of the school dies and a new one is appointed—the institution goes on. A disciple circle, on the other hand, does not transcend its principals. Disciples meet with a master and study with him. There may be a fixed curriculum; the master may have teaching assistants; the group may meet in a special building. But when the master dies, the disciple circle disbands. Some of the disciples will attach themselves to a new master. Others may consider themselves no longer in need of a master and may even take on students of their own. What I have in mind is a relationship similar to that of a group of apprentices and a master craftsman . . . It should also be noted that not only "disciples," i.e., advanced students, but also beginning students could be taught in the way described. Elementary education could also be organized on a "free-enterprise" basis rather than in institutionalized, community-run schools. [pp. 267–268]

In other words, being able to have a close relationship with one's teacher, being able to model oneself not only on that teacher's intellectual pattern, but his personal pattern, as well, was a hallmark of Babylonian education.

Our passage seems to suggest that we should learn *gemara* from one teacher so that we do not become confused, but that we learn *svara* by experiencing as many teachers as possible. It also suggests a balance. We must treasure what we receive as well as our own insights. Too often, we tend toward one extreme or another: either wanting to learn only what past generations have to tell us or only wanting to hear our own insights. The former sort makes of received learning a golden calf, while the latter makes of our own egos a god. Either way, without that balance, we can come close to making out of Torah an idol and perverting its very purpose.

We have one more exposition of Psalm 1, which shows us how to study Torah in a very concrete way:

**GEMARA (19b):** "By streams of water" (Psalms 1:3)—Said R. Tanhum bar Hanilai: [This implies that] one should divide one's years [of study] into three [and devote] one third of them to Scripture, one third to Mishnah, and one third to Talmud. But does a man know the tenure of his life?—What is meant is that [he should apply this practice to] every day [of his life].

Exactly what material should we study? "Torah" is a pretty big category when you consider that it includes all of Scripture, Mishnah, *Tosefta*, Midrash, and the Talmuds and the law that has subsequently been developed from them. One could spend one's whole life on one small part of that material alone. So what do we do? We should divide our daily study time and cover the three main rubrics: Scripture, Mishnah, and Gemara. Indeed, that is exactly what the preliminary service for each morning's prayers contains. First, we recite the priestly benediction (Numbers 6:24–26), then we learn the first mishnah from tractate *Peah*, which lists good deeds we are to do, and then we learn a piece of Gemara adapted from *B. Shabbat* 127a, which is an exposition, of sorts, on *M. Peah*'s list. In this way, each day, we study a bit of the three genres of literature mandated by the sages.

Of course, it's not enough just to study Torah; we must live it as well. In this extremely famous exposition, we learn the importance of observing one of the most important—and one of the most difficult—set of mitzvot: the laws of *lashon harah*, that is, the laws against gossiping.

> **GEMARA (19b):** Rabbi Alexandri was once calling out: Who wants life? Who wants life? All the people came and gathered round him saying: Give us life! He said to them: "Who is the man who desires life and loves days that he may see good therein? Keep your tongue from evil and your lips from speaking guile, depart from evil and do good, seek peace and pursue it" (Psalms 34:13–15). Lest a person say: I kept my tongue from evil and my lips from speaking guile, I may therefore indulge in sleep, Scripture says: "Turn from evil and do good." By "good" naught but Torah is meant; as it is said, "For I have given you a *good* doctrine, forsake you not my *Torah*."

This exposition is justly famous and points to a deep truth of spiritual journeys. As we make our way towards God's will in our lives, first we rid ourselves of destructive habits and practices. We get out of abusive relationships. We quit drinking, smoking, or abusing substances. We stop speaking badly about others. But just ridding ourselves of negatives is not enough. We have to add positive aspects to our lives through the study of Torah.

Spiritual development is often explained through the metaphor of climbing a mountain and this is partly correct because we move upward through the journey. However, a better metaphor might be a spiral staircase. We keep encountering the same issues time after time, but at a higher level at each go-round. We are never done dealing with issues of pain or self-esteem, for example. However, if we rid our lives of negativism and become suffused with the spirit of Torah, we can elevate ourselves as we deal with these issues.

From these selections from the Gemara, we see that, to a great extent, the Gemara is spiritualizing the concrete agenda of the Mishnah. The Mishnah focuses on times, dates, places, and persons associated with idolatry. The Gemara focuses on the ways Jews can deal spiritually with such manifestations of idolatry. The Gemara clearly asserts that God is just, the one True Judge. The Gemara also plainly discloses the ways Jews suffer martyrdom at the hands of idolaters for the sake of Torah. And the Gemara shows how study can be the source of redemption. With these three maxims, the Gemara explains the essence of Judaism in the world: it claims (1) there is order and faithfulness in Jews' relationship with God; (2) that people nonetheless suffer; and (3) that people can still achieve inner peace despite that suffering, especially by studying Torah. In essence, then, the Gemara is explaining and justifying Jewish monotheism as the most powerful weapon in any fight to combat idolatry.

# 2

# Where Are the Borders?

"**W**hy is it," some ninth- and tenth-grade students once asked me, "that each time we go out on a date with a non-Jew our parents say, 'Don't get serious, now!'?" "Because," I answered, "your parents don't want you to marry them." A flash of recognition appeared on their faces. Their parents' ambivalence was clear. They did not want to prohibit interdating altogether, yet they did not feel entirely comfortable with it, either.

**Where Do We Draw the Line?**

Where do we draw the line? It's pretty easy to say, "We won't have a Christmas tree." But what about the rest of the time? What about interdating and other everyday contacts with non-Jews? Where do we stop? At dating? At trips together to the mall? At not using non-Jewish doctors or dentists? The sages struggled with these issues just as we do today. It is very difficult, if not impossible, to pin down the exact action of which we can say, "This is where we should stop." Only in hindsight can we tell that if we had stopped contact with the non-Jewish world at a certain point, an intermarriage or conversion to Christianity would not have occurred. So the sages search for the boundary within which contact with the non-Jewish world can safely take place that would simultaneously allow the Jewish people to reap the benefits of contact with that world.

Rather than using the metaphor of drawing a line in the sand for making appropriate boundaries for a Jewish community, perhaps we might more fruitfully consider the eye of a hurricane. The center is so strong that it either draws in peripheral masses or throws off those too weakly attached. But it is the dynamic, strong quality of the center that determines the robustness of the phenomenon. So it is with Jewish communities (indeed, it is so with each individual). When they are strong, clearly focused, and functioning healthfully they naturally draw people toward the center and threaten, and therefore repulse, those who are very weakly attached.

In this chapter, the Mishnah and Gemara continue to diverge. The Mishnah systematically limits interactions with idolaters, particularly when one is vulnerable, such as when one is traveling or in pain. The Gemara takes a more empathetic view of those in need. It allows needs to motivate contact with the idolatrous world and provides ways of doing so that do not violate the integrity of Judaism or the Jewish community. The Gemara systematically mitigates against the Mishnah's strictness.

The first thing the Mishnah makes clear is that one should not sleep with idolaters, that is, literally sleep with them or be in a position wherein someone could think sexual intercourse is taking place.

MISHNAH (22a): One should not place cattle in idolaters' inns, because they are suspected of immoral practice [with them]. And a woman should not be alone with them, because they are suspected of lewdness, and a person should not be alone with them, because they are suspected of shedding blood.

The emotion that underlies these prohibitions seems to be fear of violence and sexual molestation. The sages evidently suspected that idolaters would sexually molest animals and women and do violence to men. Therefore, they considered it best to avoid situations in which harm might come to Jews.

It seems unlikely that the majority of idolaters had sexual relations with animals or were rapists or murderers under normal circumstances. (Similarly, those who colluded with the

Nazis were also probably not rapists and murderers under normal circumstances but became so in the atmosphere Nazism created.) What could have caused the sages to fear idolaters so greatly? Sometimes, when there may be a predisposition to disapprove of another group, all we must hear of is one negative incident in order to say, "Be careful of group X, they habitually do bad behavior Y." And, as we saw in Chapter One, the sages experienced horrible tortures at the hands of the civil authorities, so every fresh outrage confirmed their predisposition. This may be the tendency the sages are exhibiting here.

When is it simply smart and cautious to be aware of what others might do and when is it "ageist," sexist, or racist to do so? Again, where does one draw the line? Should a woman not enter an elevator alone when a man or men are in it? Women are frequently warned against such behavior, even though it is sexist. Certainly, most men that a woman would encounter in an elevator are not robbers or rapists. However, enough of them are that prudence demands one not be alone with them in an elevator. This sort of cautiousness, which borders on discrimination, is what we will find a great deal of in this chapter. It is as if the sages of the Mishnah are giving the most cautious advice possible to ensure the safety of members of the Jewish community, just as urban dwellers today share rules of safety with each other. The Gemara adds to this sort of "safety advice," while softening the Mishnah's categorical ruling:

> **GEMARA (25b):** "A person should not be alone with them." Our Rabbis taught: If a Jew happens to be overtaken by an idolater while on the road, he should let him walk on his right. Rabbi Yishmael the son of Rabbi Yohanan ben Berokah says: [If the heathen is armed] with a sword, he should be allowed to walk on the right; if with a stick, to his [the Jew's] left. If they are ascending or descending, let not the Jew be lower and the idolater higher, but let the Jew be higher and the idolater lower. And a Jew should not bend down before him, lest he smash his skull. If [the idolater asks] him [the Jew] whither he is going, he should say [towards a place] beyond his actual destination, just as our father Jacob acted towards the wicked Esau; as it is written, "Until I come unto my lord to Seir" (Genesis 33:14), and it is

written [after it], "And Jacob journeyed to Sukkot" (Genesis 33:17).

Now we can see the difference between the idealized, but unattainable, world of the Mishnah and the more practical reality the Gemara describes. The Mishnah says, "Never be alone with idolaters." Such a prescription is unachievable or, to achieve it, one would have to live a totally isolated life that was not feasible then or now. The Gemara is much more practical. It recognizes that there will be contact between Jews and idolaters and tries to give practical advice on how to minimize possible harm during these contacts. We must also remember that travel then was not what travel is now. There were no cars with locked doors, cellular phones with which to call for help, or credit cards that could replace cash carried on a person. To be traveling was to be vulnerable.

The Gemara, with its inward focus, addresses the issue of a traveler's feeling of vulnerability and how to minimize it. Again, this is very similar to the way women are adjured to deal with their urban environments. They are to be aware of their vulnerability but use vigilance and wit to overcome their disadvantage. The practical portent of the Gemara's rules are as follows. It was assumed that the Jewish person in these examples was right handed. Therefore, having the idolater on his right side meant the Jew could more easily ward off an attack. Apparently in those days swords were worn on the left side and sticks on the right. Therefore, Rabbi Yohanan suggests that one walk on the side closest to the idolater's weapon so that the Jew can quickly foil an attack should one begin.

The biblical example comes from Jacob and Esau's reunion many years after Jacob stole his brother's blessing. Jacob is fearful of his older brother, but Esau's anger has long since waned. Nonetheless, Jacob is not anxious to travel with Esau, who has graciously suggested that they travel together (Genesis 33:12). So Jacob makes the excuse that his children demand a slower pace and tells Esau to go on ahead to Seir (i.e, Edom, directly south of the Dead Sea), while he, Jacob, will follow more slowly behind him. It is then reported (Genesis 33:17) that Jacob travels to Sukkot, which is on the west bank of the Jordan river about half way between the Kinneret (the Sea of Galilee) and the Dead Sea. Jacob could have been making his way slowly to Seir. However, the sages' interpretation of his actions, that Jacob is telling his older brother that he will follow him all the way to the Dead Sea while actually stopping almost as soon as possible (this conversation between the brothers takes place at Pni'el, just east of Sukkot, across the Jordan), seems quite likely. Note that Esau is called "the wicked one." His actions in the actual Torah tale are quite noble. But because Esau is seen as the progenitor and prototype of Rome and its idolatry, he is characterized as wicked. Whatever Jacob did to preserve himself against his brother's might was warranted, in the sages' view.

Perhaps these sound like suspicious or unkind rules. However, we have only to look at our own society to realize that similar suggestions are directed at travelers on a regular basis. For instance, we are advised not to drive rental cars with stickers that identify them as such. We are to be aware of persons wearing heavy coats on balmy days lest they be concealing a weapon, and so forth.

We, like the sages, live in a society that has in it a component of fear. We should bear in mind that this is but one of many, many tractates of the Talmud and that the sages were not obsessed with, nor dominated by, the risks of their world. On the other hand, they took what were considered prudent precautions against those risks, and this is one of the tractates of the Talmud that deals with that topic most extensively. Their tactics are the tactics most people would use and what most people are advised to do: avoid trouble. It is better to side-step situations that are risky than have to deal with a situation that has gotten out of hand. Note that Jews are not advised to become "Rambos" and turn violent themselves. Rather, they are to avoid situations that might lead to violence and not present the opportunity for violence to occur.

## Healing and the Idolatrous World

The perception of idolaters as the enemy is clearly present in the following mishnah:

MISHNAH (26a): A Jewish woman should not act as midwife to an idolater, because she would be delivering a child for idolatry. But a [woman] idolater may act as midwife to a Jewish woman. A Jewish woman should not nurse the child of an idolater, but an idolater may nurse a Jewish child in the [Jewish woman's] premises.

We are not to foster the expansion of idolatry in any way, according to this mishnah. This is a very clean, clear set of rules. As usual, the Gemara reveals a much more complicated world where blunt refusals of aid, as outlined in the mishnah, would lead to a great deal of ill will.

GEMARA (26a): A Jewish woman may act as a midwife to an idolater woman for payment, but not for free. Said Rav Yosef: Payment is permitted to prevent ill feeling. Rav Yosef had a mind to say that even on the Sabbath it is permitted to act as midwife to a heathen for payment, so as to avoid ill feeling. Abaye said to him: She [the Jewish woman] can make the excuse, "Only for our own, who keep the Sabbath, may we violate it, but we do not violate the Sabbath for those who do not keep it." Rav Yosef also had a mind to say that nursing for payment should be allowed because of ill-feeling. Said to him Abaye: She [the Jewish woman] can, if she is unmarried, make the excuse, "I want to get married." If she is married [she can say], "I will not degrade myself before my husband."

The Gemara allows, under limited circumstances, what the Mishnah forbids. This is a classic illustration of the principle, "The big print giveth and the small print taketh away." The sages of the Gemara understand that a Jewish midwife's refusal to aid a suffering idolater in labor would create ill will toward the Jewish community. Therefore, they allow Jewish midwives to aid idolaters by professionalizing the relationship; the midwives do it as a job but not as volunteers. Money provides some social, religious, and psychological distance in this relationship, just as it does today in the healing arts. There is a legitimate, business basis for the transaction. What happens, however, when a Jewish midwife would have to violate the Sabbath to help an idolatrous woman in labor? Rav Yosef would tend to allow it while Abaye suggests that the Jewish midwife make an excuse in order to avoid desecrating the Sabbath. (Naturally, the Sabbath may be desecrated to help a Jewish woman in labor.)

A similar discrepancy of opinion surrounds Jewish women being wetnurses for idolaters' babies. Rav Yosef and Abaye hold to their positions. Rav Yosef suggests that it be permitted on a "professional" basis while Abaye urges Jewish women to make some plausible excuse. Note that neither urges that the Jewish women flatly refuse. Interestingly, Abaye's answer suggests that an unmarried woman would have had a baby and would be waiting to get married. Perhaps he is thinking, for example, of a woman widowed while she was pregnant. She would want to refuse to wetnurse in order that she could be married and have another child from her husband. Either that, or Abaye is simply making theoretical statements that can be generalized: when refusing to participate in the non-Jewish world we should give a plausible excuse that will not cause offense. We see once more how the Mishnah draws sharp boundaries and how the Gemara is more aware of the effect these boundaries will have on peoples' attitudes and relationships. The Mishnah's idealistic vision of the world is tempered by the Gemara's need to have actual Jews live in a real world. The Gemara forms the bridge, as it were, between the ideal and the real.

Perhaps the most common modern dilemma that is analogous to these is what to do when store clerks wish us "Merry Christmas!" Should we reply, "I don't celebrate Christmas"? Or should we simply say, "Thank you"? We might imagine that Rav Yosef would side with the latter option and that Abaye might favor the former, or an even milder version of it. What is clear is that separating ourselves from the non-Jewish world is put forward as an important value by the Mishnah. That value is counterbalanced in the Gemara by the need to maintain goodwill with the non-Jewish communities that surround us. Any one-sided approach to the problem is untenable: both views are correct and incorrect if taken to the extreme. The key is to find the right balance.

In continuing to "fine tune" the ways we may and may not relate to idolaters, the Mishnah now outlines another set of rules for a time when a Jew and an idolater would be in close contact with each other, that is, in a healing situation or in a barber shop.

> **MISHNAH (27a):** We may allow them to heal us when the healing [is paid for by] money, but not healing [paid for by] souls (*n'fashot*); nor should we have our hair cut by them in any place. [These are the] words of Rabbi Meir. And the sages say: in a public place it is permitted, but not when the two persons are alone.

How is one to understand this mishnah? The commentators take the "healing of money" to refer to one's livestock and the "healing of the soul" to refer to one's self (Albek Mishnah and Rambam, there). Rambam, in his commentary on the Mishnah, takes pains to point out that the law does not follow Rabbi Meir in this matter.

The mishnah continues exploring the ways Jews and non-Jews can relate to each other in times of great need such as in illness. One is allowed to have one's animals healed by an idolater. There is a dispute, though, as to whether we are allowed to use non-Jewish doctors. Rabbi Meir forbids it, but the sages permit it in a public place when there are many people about since the presence of witnesses would prevent any attack on the part of the physician.

How can we understand this? Obviously, the Mishnah isn't so worried about molestation of animals that the sages would deny them healing at the hands of an idolater. But the Mishnah is still worried about a Jew and an idolater being alone together, particularly in a situation wherein the Jew is in a vulnerable position. Imagine how you'd feel if you walked into a doctor's office and found her to be a neo-Nazi with swastikas draped over the reception desk. Admittedly, this scenario is far-fetched, but it gives you an idea of what the sages were worried about. The fear underlying this mishnah is that the balance between the desire for physical life and for one's relationship with God or the Jewish people might come into conflict and that one should remain loyal to one's eternal relationships.

The Gemara illustrates the problem underlying the mishnah with a story about a Jew and a heretical faith healer. In this story, human, physical needs are pitted against a person's relationship with God and faithful adherence to monotheism.

> **GEMARA (27b):** It once happened to Ben Dama, the son of Rabbi Yishmael's sister, that he was bitten by a snake, and Jacob [a *min*], a native of K'far S'khanya, came to heal him, and Rabbi Yishmael did not let him. And he [Dama] said, "Rabbi Yishmael my brother, let him, so that I may be healed by him. And I will [even] cite a verse from the Torah that he is permitted [to heal me]." But he did not manage to complete his saying, when his soul departed and he died. Rabbi Ishmael exclaimed, "Happy are you, Ben Dama, for you were pure in body and your soul left you in purity; nor have you transgressed the words of your colleagues, who would say, 'He who breaks through a fence, a snake shall bite him' (Ecclesiastes 10:8)." . . .
>
> The Master said: "Nor have you transgressed the words of your colleagues, who said, 'He who breaks through a fence, a snake shall bite him' (Ecclesiastes 10:8). But a snake did indeed sting him!—The bite of the snake [which is inflicted upon those transgressing the words] of the Rabbis is such as can never be cured.
>
> Now, what is it that he might have said? "He shall live by them" (Leviticus 18:5), but not die by them. And Rabbi Yishmael, [what objection would he raise to that]? This is only meant when in private, but not in public; for it has been taught: Rabbi Yishmael used to say (*B. Sanhedrin* 74a): Whence can we deduce that if they say to a person, "Worship the idol and you will not be killed," that he may worship it so as not to be killed? [Because] Scripture says, "he shall live by them," but not die by them; you might take this to mean even in public, therefore Scripture says, "And you shall not profane My holy name" (Leviticus 22:32).

Let us examine this passage in its two parts: the story and the later commentary on it. The story is one in which the tension put forth theoretically in the mishnah is embodied within Rabbi Yishmael and his nephew. Rabbi Yishmael will not allow his nephew to be cured by Jacob (identified as one who heals in Jesus' name in the parallel text, *Tosefta Chullin* 2:22–23). Ben Dama pleads with his uncle to allow Jacob to heal him, but dies before he can bring the scriptural proof that would have supported this leniency. Rabbi Yishmael rejoices at the triumph

of Dama's immortal soul for he has not transgressed the fence
that the sages placed around the Torah that, the verse says, will
lead to a scorpion bite if breached.

Now, the later commentators notice the obvious conun-
drum: he *was* bitten by a serpent even though he did not
transgress the fence! The discrepancy is resolved by making the
sting spoken of here refer to the eternal sting of punishment in
the World to Come which, unlike a physical serpent's sting,
brings everlasting pain and loss of life in the world beyond
physical death. The sages commenting on this story thus recon-
cile themselves to Ben Dama's loss of life here, counting it better
to have lost temporal life than eternal life.

They now try to guess what text it might have been that
Ben Dama would have brought in his support. The obvious one
would be the injunction "to live by them" (Leviticus 18:5),
generally interpreted as, "transgress one precept and live to
observe many more rather than die." (*Sifra* Leviticus, Acharei
Mot 13.) This is a most well-known interpretation of the verse
and a standard principle of Jewish law: the obligation to
preserve life is paramount and ritual rules may be disregarded
if they constitute a danger to one's life (B. *Yoma* 85b). However,
Rabbi Yishmael would probably say that here, as with everything else, one must achieve a balance. Life does not reign
absolute. Some things, if done, make life a living death. Saving
your life by committing sexual sins, such as adultery or incest,
murdering someone else so that you may not be murdered, or
curing yourself through idolatry are forbidden (see B. *Sanhedrin*
74a and B. *Pesachim* 25a–b). So Rabbi Yishmael, the sages suggest,
would make it clear that one may not cure oneself through
idolatry in public because it profanes God's name. In private,
however, one may worship an idol in order to avoid being slain
since this does not publicly defame God (B. *Sanhedrin* 74a).

This passage leaves us with many questions. Did Rabbi
Yishmael forbid the treatment only because it would have
constituted a public victory for Jacob? Was it because Jacob was
a well-known faith healer that he ruled as he did? Perhaps he
knew the wound was incurable and the appeal to Jacob would
simply be a meaningless betrayal of Dama's whole life. Or did
Rabbi Yishmael truly prefer that his nephew die rather than take

part in idolatry? Is there something worse than death? Are there things worth dying for? The sages, by including this story in the Gemara in this way, indicate that Rabbi Yishmael acted correctly in this matter. There *are* things worth dying for . . . and, in this case, Judaism was one of them.

## It Ain't Over till It's Over . . . Then It's Over

As the Gemara endeavors to elucidate what sort of contact with idolaters is permitted and forbidden, it also struggles with the fact that there were (and are today) a range of Jews. In this short passage they differentiate between misbehaving Jews.

> **GEMARA (26b):** It has been stated: [In regard to the term apostate (*mumar*)] there is a divergence of opinion between Rav Aha and Ravina. One said that [he who eats forbidden food] to satisfy his appetite, is a *mumar* and [he who does it] to provoke is a *min*; while the other said that even [one who does it] to provoke is merely a *mumar*. And who is a *min*?—One who actually worships idols.

What is the difference between a *mumar*, a Jew who ignores Jewish law, and a *min*, whose closest modern-day equivalent is a Jew for Jesus? The term *min* is most often used to denote a Jew who has become a Christian although in this passage it simply means a Jew who became an idol worshiper. Clearly, all these terms were fluid and precise definitions for each category will be difficult to elucidate (see also, for example, in this tractate pp. 32b–33a). Today's terms for designating kinds of Jews are likewise quite flexible. One person's definition of Reform, Conservative, or Orthodox Judaism might be quite different from another's.

In this passage, Rav Aha suggests that a *mumar* is one who, if no other food is available, will eat nonkosher meat out of desire and that a *min* is one who will eat nonkosher meat even if kosher food is available, in order to make people angry. Ravina suggests that an apostate is one who eats nonkosher meat even if kosher food is available while a *min* is a Jew who actually worships idols. Ravina's ruling is actually the more lenient in that one must do something quite serious to be categorized as a follower of another religion as opposed to merely being a lapsed Jew. Ravina's system condemns fewer people to the category *min*, which is outside the Jewish people. The *mumar*, while no saint, is still a Jew. These opinions are summarized in table 2–1.

**Table 2–1.**

|          | *Mumar*                             | *Min*          |
|----------|-------------------------------------|----------------|
| Rav Aha  | eats nonkosher meat out of desire   | to anger       |
| Ravina   | eats nonkosher meat to anger        | worships idols |

Notice how important internal states and motivations are to these sages. It really matters why a person ate the nonkosher meat.

When does a Jew step outside the bounds of the Jewish community? When she eats *treif* with no justifiable reason or when she denies the central creed of Judaism: that there is only one God? Is it mitzvot or theology that makes the difference? Today, when so many people do not keep kosher, probably a majority of the Jewish people would be called apostates (*mumarim*) according to Rav Aha's definition. Perhaps Ravina's rule is more appropriate for today's Jewish community. Even the most unobservant Jew still probably believes that there is only one God. As long as a Jew holds to the tenets expressed in the Shema, that Jew is still in the orbit of Jewish law and lore. But once a Jew renounces the idea of monotheism, she has floated away from Judaism's influence altogether.

And how is such a Jew treated? This Jew has become, for the sages, the "enemy." In fact, if a *min* is stranded in a pit, a Jew is not obligated to bring him up out of that pit. (Characteristically for the Gemara [26b], there is a difference of opinion on that topic: Rav Yosef feels that one should help the *min* out of the pit for a fee while Abaye feels a Jew should make an excuse for not doing so. They are consistent in their differences!) This leads us to the important and painful question of how we are to treat such Jews today. Are idolaters the enemy? Are Jews for Jesus?

Should you help them? Or are Jews who eat nonkosher food the enemy? Is it productive to think in terms of "the enemy"? How else might we think about those issues? One thing is certain: these questions are as alive for us today as they were for the sages some fifteen hundred years ago.

When does one give up hope that a person will be faithful to the Jewish religion? And to what extent may a person participate, even indirectly, in idol worship? That is what the Gemara addresses in this passage.

> GEMARA (32b–33a): "With idolaters going on a pilgrimage it is forbidden to have any business transactions" (Mishnah 29b). Shmuel said: With idolaters going on a pilgrimage it is forbidden [to transact business] on their journey there, for they will go and offer thanks to the idols. [But] on [their] way back, it is permitted, because what has been has been. If a Jew goes on such a pilgrimage [to idols], it is permitted [to deal with him] on his journey there, for he may change his mind and not go. But on the way back, it is forbidden, for as (33a) he has already become attached to it he will go again and again.
>
> But has it not been taught: It is forbidden [to do any business transactions] with a Jew going on a pilgrimage of idolatry either on his journey there or back?— Rav Ashi said: That refers to an apostate Israelite (*mumar*), who is sure to go.

The Mishnah, in its usual way, states things broadly: one may not transact business with idolaters going to one of their festivals for fear that the money you put in the idolater's hands may become part of his idol worshiping. However, the Gemara adds on the way back, "what has been, has been" and there is no changing it. With a Jew, on the other hand, we may do business with her on the way to the pagan festival as we hope that she may still have a change of heart. However, on the way home, having seen her worship idols, we assume she is fully corrupted and we should refuse to contribute monetarily to her idol worship by doing business with her. Now, what should we do in the case of a Jew who we *know* is going to worship idols (the *mumar*)? With this Jew, we should do no business coming or going. He's relinquished his status as a Jew with whom we

might have done business on the way there and we certainly
don't have the attitude of "what has been, has been" on the way
home. Notice that in this passage the *mumar* worships idols
habitually. As noted above, these terms were flexible and subject
to idiosyncratic usage.

Today, this sort of issue is brought most wrenchingly to the
fore with the topic of intermarriage. What do you do with a
couple contemplating an interfaith wedding? Do you attempt to
talk them out of it up to the time they walk down the aisle? Or
do you take the attitude that "what has been, has been" and
refuse to attend the wedding but, once the ceremony is over, go
to the reception? Or do you refuse to have anything to do with
them once the intermarriage is a certain thing? This concept of
"before and after" is described in rabbinic literature with the two
words *l'khatchilah* and *b'di'avad*, which Rabbi Steinsaltz (1989)
defines as follows:

> *b'di'avad*: Literally, "it having been done." A situation where
> the correctness or validity of an action is being considered after it
> has taken place, as opposed to *l'khatchilah (ab initio)*, where the
> correctness or validity of the action is being considered *before* it
> takes place. [p. 109]

Using this sort of logic, we might say that we should
protest an intermarriage up to the point when it has taken place.
Once it has been done, we might decide to simply accept it.
However, there is also a principle that states that even once
something has been done, it is still an invalid act. Nonetheless,
timing and the existence of a *fait accompli* can have some
influence on our thinking in some cases. Is the model of the Jew
on the way to, and on the way back from, the idolatrous
pilgrimage a useful one for framing this dilemma? Should we
cut off relations after an intermarriage has taken place? Or shall
we say of the non-Jew in this case, "what has been has been" and
make a relationship with him or her? The paradigm of the
pilgrimage may be a useful one for clarifying these issues.

## Classification Systems of Jews

The sages had as many, or more, ways of classifying Jews as
do today's sociologists. The sages' categories, however, were

based on different criteria than current systems'. One way they classified Jews was through their bloodlines. These were called the *'asarah yochasin*, the ten lineage categories:

1. *Cohanim*: Priests

2. *L'vi'im*: Levites

3. *Yisra'elim*: Israelites

4. *Chalalim*: Children of priests disqualified from the priesthood because their father's married women not allowed to them (e.g., divorcees).

5. Converts

6. Freed slaves

7. Illegitimate children (products of an adulterous union)

8. *N'tinim*: A descendant of the Gibeonites who converted to Judaism against whom Joshua declared that they were *mamzeirim* (illegitimate) and therefore, Jews were not allowed to marry them. (There are none of these today.)

9. *Sh'tukim*: Children whose father is unknown.

10. *Asufim*: Foundlings; children whose father and mother are unknown.

This classification system is found in Mishnah Kiddushin 4:1. The first three groups are people with acceptable blood lines. Category four are people whose bloodlines disqualify them from marrying priests but are fine otherwise. Categories 5 and 6 have no bloodlines to speak of within this system. Categories 7 and 8 have bad blood lines and we are lacking crucial information about the bloodlines of those in categories 9 and 10. The first three categories can marry among themselves. Categories 2–6 may marry each other. Categories 5–8 may marry among themselves. However, categories 9 and 10 cannot even marry people in their own category lest they inadvertently marry a relative, but they may marry people in categories 5–8 to whom they would have no blood ties (Steinsaltz, *Reference Guide*, p. 243).

The system outlined above is one based on bloodlines, which reflects the priestly outlook. Bloodlines were of paramount importance to priests as this was what distinguished a Priest, from a Levite, from an Israelite. One's position was determined by one's blood.

The sages developed a system that reflected Jewish life after the destruction of the Temple. This system depended not on blood but on learning and observance of the mitzvot. In the sages' system, one could be in the following categories:

1. *Amora*: One who translated and amplified the lecture of a great sage.

2. *Chakham*: A sage who discussed *mishnayot* and *baraitot*.

3. *Tanna*: One who repeated *mishnayot* and *baraitot* from memory for the sages to discuss.

4. *Chaveir*: One who was devoted to the precise observance of the mitzvot, especially taking care to observe the laws of the "Jewish taxes" from agricultural products and the rules of ritual purity. The sages were all in this category, but some lay Israelites were, as well. A *chaveir's* word was considered trustworthy with regard to whether some produce had been tithed or an item was ritually clean.

5. *Am Ha'arets*: An ignorant person who was not scrupulous in observing the commandments. This is the opposite of a *chaveir*. Such a person's word was not accepted with regard to matters of ritual purity and agricultural "taxes."

6. *Mumar*: An apostate Jew as outlined, above.

7. *Min*: Either a sinning Jew or a Jew who became a Christian or a Zoroastrian.

8. *Ger Toshav*: A resident alien who has accepted some of the laws of Judaism. A non-Jew who wishes to live

permanently in the Land of Israel must accept certain mitzvot, as discussed in the passage, below, in Chapter 5.

[Steinsaltz 1989, p. 104, 116, 142, 188, 241, and 177]

Among the general population, the relevant categories would be the *chaveir* and *am ha'arets*.

The sages assumed that a person was a *chaveir* until disqualified, and even the members of that person's house, too, were considered reliable in the matters about which *chaveirim* cared until they were disqualified.

> **GEMARA (39a):** Said Shmuel: The wife of a *chaveir* is like a *chaveir*, for our Rabbis taught: The wife of a *chaveir* is like a *chaveir*, the slave of a *chaveir* is like a *chaveir*. When a *chaveir* dies his wife, children, and members of his household remain in that state of confidence until they give grounds for suspicion. . . . Rabbi Shimon ben Elazar [said]: It happened that a woman married to a *chaveir* used to tie the phylacteries upon his arm. She [afterward] married a tax-collector and she used to tie the tax seals upon his arm.

One of the least-beloved figures in Jewish life was the tax collector. The case that brings this teaching to the fore here is one where a man has brought the blue thread for his tallit (the *tsitsit*) from the widow of a *chaveir*. This blue colored wool (*tekhelet*) was so expensive that merchants tended to cheat and use indigo as a dye instead of the proper color made from the murex snail (*B. Baba Metsia* 61b). Is she to be considered a reliable source of *tekhelet* or, since her husband has died, is she to be considered untrustworthy? Shmuel teaches that anyone in a *chaveir*'s family is considered as trustworthy as the *chaveir*. The sages agree with Shmuel and assume that a household will have a homogeneous religious practice. Rabbi Shimon ben Elazar's example, however, provides a counterpoint: this woman, when married to a *chaveir*, would help him wind the leather straps of the *tefillin* around his arm. Then, when she was married to a tax collector, she would wind the tax seals on his arm in almost the same way. Thus this woman mindlessly wound for her husbands whatever needed winding and did not do so out of any conviction in either case. She, however, appears to be the exception and it would seem that the general assumption was that women helped to participate in mitzvot with intention.

In the particular case here, the woman has no motives of her own. However, our own experience, and the sages' ruling, as well, seem to indicate that a woman married to a *chaveir*, and the children they educated together, were likely to internalize the *chaveir*'s systematically stringent approach to the mitzvot. Imagine the analogous situation today. It would be quite unlikely that the widow and children of an extremely observant Jew would suddenly eat nonkosher food or drive on Shabbat once the husband and father was dead. It is more likely that people then, as now, tended to marry within their categories because they were simply more compatible.

One of the most often used schemes for characterizing the American Jewish community today is that of Daniel J. Elazar (1976). In Elazar's system, Jews are identified as follows:

1.  Integral Jews who live according to Jewish rhythm.

2.  Participants who are involved in Jewish life on a regular basis.

3.  Associated Jews who affiliate with Jewish institutions in some concrete way.

4.  Contributors and consumers, who give money and/or utilize the services of Jewish institutions from time to time.

5.  Peripherals who are recognizably Jewish in some way but completely uninvolved in Jewish life.

6.  Repudiators who deny their Jewishness.

7.  Quasi-Jews whose Jewish status is unclear. [p. 72]

Like the sages with regard to *chaveirim* and *amei ha'arets*, we expect different behavior from Integral Jews than from Peripherals. For example, we'd find it difficult to see how an "Integral

Jew" and a "Peripheral" could marry without a great degree of conflict regarding religious practice. This does not mean that one cannot move from one category to another, but that proximity and domestic peace make it more likely that people will remain within their groups.

We *are* influenced by those around us. It therefore stands to reason that we are capable of influencing those around us as well. We may do so in ways of which we're not aware. If you are walking to Shabbat services, people driving past may see you and be influenced to eventually do the same. You are not trying to influence them; you would simply be making your way to synagogue. Nonetheless, you would be serving as a role model. Our surroundings, and those in them, do make a difference. If one has as a goal greater depth in one's Jewish life, one could use the categorization scheme the sages put forth (or those developed by their modern, sociological counterparts) and try to place oneself with those who will exert a positive influence on one's Jewish practice.

## How to Prevent Intermarriages

The problem of intermarriage in the Jewish community is not a new one. Despite the romantic notions that previous generations of Jews were utterly faithful and that the current generation is especially prone to assimilation, a close look at the texts reveals that intermarriage was a problem in the sages' days, as well, and that they took measures to prevent it.

> **MISHNAH (35b):** These are the articles of idolaters that are prohibited but the prohibition is not one prohibiting benefit [from them] . . . their bread and oil—Rabbi and his court permitted the oil. . . .

> **GEMARA (35b):** One time Rabbi went out into a field, and an idolater brought before him a loaf baked in a large oven from about two gallons of flour. Rabbi said: How beautiful is this bread! Why did the Sages see fit to prohibit it! "Why should the Sages have thought fit [to prohibit it]?!" Because of [inter]marriages!

Bread and oil were two of the main foodstuffs of the ancient world. A Jew might not be able to consume idolaters' bread and oil but could trade in these foodstuffs and sell them to other idolaters. The sages prohibited Jews from eating idolaters' bread as a precaution against intermarriage.

Now, why would the sages have prevented their oil from being consumed by Jews? Olive oil was a major industry in the ancient Near East as, indeed, it is today. Large stone processing vats were used to press the oil. Archaeological investigations of such processing centers indicate that they may have been run, at least in part, by priests of idolatrous religions, for shrines have been found in the buildings associated with the production of olive oil. Thus, the sages may have prohibited Jews from consuming this oil because they feared that it was tainted by idolatrous worship.

In general, it would be difficult to marry someone with whom you could not eat. The sages were evidently aware of the principle: "You can't marry someone you don't date." This principle works in two directions: if a Jew does not date a non-Jew, then the Jew cannot marry a non-Jew, and if a Jew does not date any Jews then the Jew cannot marry any Jews. By ruling that one is not allowed to eat idolaters' bread, the sages greatly reduced the likelihood of intermarriage.

### Don't Make Laws People Won't Follow

The Gemara now goes on to illustrate the limits of rabbinic authority in those days. Even though the sages had prohibited Jews from using idolaters' oil, apparently few Jews paid heed to their interdiction:

> **GEMARA (36a):** Our masters sat and made investigation concerning [the use of heathens'] oil [and found] that its prohibition had not spread among the majority of Jews. They [thereupon] relied upon the words of Rabban Shimon ben Gamliel and on the words of Rabbi Eliezer bar Tsadok, who would say: We make no decree upon the community unless the majority are able to abide by it. For Rav Adda bar Ahavah said: What scriptural verse [supports this rule]? (36b) "You are cursed with the curse;

for you rob Me, even this whole nation" (Malachai 3:9). If the whole nation has [accepted an ordinance, then the curse that is the penalty for its infraction] does apply, otherwise it does not.

Here we have a classic example of a religious elite making a decree and the majority of Jews ignoring that decree. In American culture, we witness such discrepancies all the time. For example, experts condemn television programming as harmful, but people continue to watch it in large numbers. Here, the sages decreed that Jews shouldn't use heathens' olive oil, but very few Jews appear to have paid attention. Rabbi Eliezer bar Tsadok's and Rabban Shimon ben Gamliel's wise ruling is then cited: it weakens the authority of the legislating body to make rules that no one follows. Idealized visions of a community are fine, but legislation must have some basis in reality and take into account the community's economic needs.

Now, we can imagine that there might be some resistance to such a notion. So it is immediately bolstered by a scriptural support. The verse from Malachai is interpreted as meaning that only when the whole nation accepts a law shall the punishment adhering to it be enforced. Otherwise, the punishment will not be brought upon the population.

Does this ruling leave the door open to sanction intermarriage? Fifty-two percent of Jews who married between 1985 and 1990 married non-Jews, so clearly a majority of Jews are not following the legislation against intermarriage (CJF 1991, 14). Not surprisingly, the sages have a concept that resolves this problem nicely. The sages recognized that there is a "core" Jewish population that lives by a Jewish calendar and observes the laws of *kashrut*, Shabbat, and ritual purity. And they also recognized that there is a group of Jews who simply don't abide by the mitzvot (see *B. Baba Metsia* 59a). They had different expectations of these two groups of people and different rules sometimes applied to them.

This chapter shows the divergence of the Mishnah from the Gemara. The Mishnah stringently limits interaction between Jews and idolaters in its ideal vision of how a Jewish community ought to work. Even in an hour of need, Jews and idolaters should shun each other lest Jews somehow contribute to idolatry. The Gemara, on the other hand, shows a sensitivity to Jews' desires to be healed by idolaters and to benefit from idolaters' goods. The Gemara, personified by Yehudah Nesiah's ambivalence, wants to partake of the goodness they see in the idolaters' world. The competing forces that operated on Jews then still function today. Jews want to maintain an authentically Jewish life while participating in the very real benefits of the world that surrounds them. The Mishnah brooks no discussion of this tension. The Gemara, with its focus on inner states, recognizes the dilemma and allows an explicit discussion of the issue, as embodied by the dying Dama's case, but also seen in Rav Yosef's and Abaye's disagreements and the way people moved from one level of observance to another. An inner attachment to Judaism is the only sure way of maintaining Jewish life. For from that inner state come all the behaviors the Mishnah wanted to legislate.

# 3

# Power Without and Within

L et's imagine that a person has been addicted to cigarettes. If this person wanted to renounce her addiction, she would not only have to get rid of the cigarettes, but everything associated with them: ashtrays, lighters, perhaps even the favorite chair she used to sit in to smoke and read. To become truly free of the addiction would mean not holding on to any item associated with that behavior. She might even ceremonially and/or publicly throw out her smoking paraphernalia to show that she was really through with her addiction. And as the cleaning and the cure progressed ever further, fewer and fewer central objects would be thrown out. In other words, first she'd throw out the cigarettes, then the ashtrays, next the lighters, and so forth. That sort of "decontamination procedure" is what is described in this chapter with regard to idols and their accouterments.

## The Biblical Basis

To understand the basis for such a decontamination procedure, we have to grasp its biblical source: the book of Deuteronomy and the "Deuteronomic revolution," which is the background for this book of the Torah. Biblical Israel was a whole nation for a very short time, during the reigns of Kings David and Solomon (1000–930 B.C.E.). After that, it split into two kingdoms: Israel in the North and Judah in the South. Each of these tiny states allied itself with the different superpowers of those days, Egypt to the South and Assyria to the North. Eventually, the northern kingdom was destroyed (723 B.C.E.) and only Judah remained, a puppet state under the thumb of the then-all-powerful Assyria (modern day Iraq). Eventually, Assyria weakened and Judah was able to reassert its independence during the rule of King Josiah (640–608 B.C.E.). Not only did Josiah expand Judah's territory but he developed Jerusalem as its cultic center. He instituted reforms designed to unify and purify the cult and rid Judah and its religious institutions of all the Assyrian trappings that had crept in during the long years of Assyrian domination. These reforms were promulgated by a "Book of the Torah" discovered in the Temple in the eighteenth year of his reign (622 B.C.E.), generally identified with the book of Deuteronomy.

Given this background of a reassertion of national identity and power along with a cleansing of the cult of all foreign influences and a centralization of it in Jerusalem, Deuteronomy's emphasis on decontaminating Judaism from idolatrous influences makes tremendous sense. One representative passage demands the utter destruction of anything linked to idolatry:

> If you shall hear tell concerning one of your cities, which the Lord your God gives you to dwell there, saying, Certain base fellows are gone out from among you and have drawn away the inhabitants of their city, saying: Let us go and serve other gods, which you have not known; then shall you inquire and search and ask diligently and, behold, if it be true, and the thing certain, that such abomination is wrought among you, you shall surely smite the inhabitants of the city with the edge of the sword, destroying it utterly, and all that is therein and the cattle thereof, with the edge of the sword. And you shall gather all the spoil of it into the midst of the broad place thereof, and shall burn with fire the city and all the spoil thereof, every bit, unto the Lord your God and it shall be a heap forever and it shall not be built again.
>
> And there shall cleave nothing of the devoted thing to your hand, that the Lord may turn from the fierceness of His anger, and show you mercy and have compassion upon you and multiply you as He has sworn unto your fathers when you shall hearken to the voice of the Lord your God, to keep all His

commandments which I command you this day, to do that which is right in the eyes of the Lord your God. [Deuteronomy 13:13–19]

The procedure for ridding the country of idolatrous influences is one we can easily imagine being duplicated in Lithuania's drive for independence from the Soviet Union. Lithuania, like ancient Judah, was a puppet state under the domination of a superpower. Having been under Soviet rule for so long, Lithuanians probably systematically took all the flags and placards, statues of Lenin, and posters proclaiming Soviet might and right and destroyed them. Anyone who displayed such materials would be taken as a traitor to the hard-won victory for independence.

### Making the Leap to Modern Times

To American Jewish eyes, the principles of Deuteronomy and the actions of Lithuanians seem distant, perhaps even bigoted. This is because we, as Americans, do not know what it is to be deprived of religious freedom and to have to swear allegiance to a flag that represents tyranny, not justice. Since we don't experience the need for religious freedom, we don't truly comprehend the motivations of Deuteronomy. Our need for religious freedom and autonomy is satisfied to such an extent that it makes it difficult for us to understand how we would react were it not a satisfied need.

To be able to truly understand this tractate, and this chapter, we almost need to visualize and fantasize what our lives would be like if we could not openly express our Judaism or our American identity, not just for a day but for our whole lives. How it would begin to grate on us, to know that who we were was not acceptable to the powers that ruled us! How we would long to be rid of our rulers and assert our identities publicly! And how gladly would we rid ourselves of all signs of our rulers and denounce those who would go back to the days and ways of oppression. These, indeed, were many of the motivations that set the American Revolution in motion.

Now that we have a better sense of the milieu that

engendered the Torah verses underlying this chapter of the Mishnah and Gemara, we can begin to study these documents. In the first chapter of this tractate, the Mishnah explored how to deal with idolatrous people at times of intense idolatry, and the Gemara examined the theological differences between monotheism and idolatry. The Mishnah's second chapter explored day-to-day interactions between Jews and idolaters, and the Gemara considered how Jews might interact with idolaters without losing their souls. Now the Mishnah moves further out from the core experience of idolatry to examine how to share space with idols, pieces of idols, buildings in which idols reside, and parts of nature (e.g., trees and hills) that have been worshiped in idolatrous ways while the Gemara considers how to remove idol worship from inside an idolater.

### Which Images Are Idols?

The first question the Mishnah addresses is, logically, how is one to treat whole idolatrous statues and which statues are to be designated as such?

> MISHNAH (40b): All images are prohibited because they are worshiped once a year. [These are the] words of Rabbi Meir. But the Sages say: [An image] is not prohibited except one that has a staff or bird or orb in its hand. Rabban Shimon ben Gamliel says: Also any [image] that has anything in its hand [is prohibited].

We have here two views. Rabbi Meir says that a Jew is prohibited from deriving benefit from any image, picture, or statue that belongs to an idolater because it is uncertain whether this image is used in idolatry. However, the sages take a more lenient view. They prohibit only those images that are portrayed as having some power. Various pagan gods were portrayed with the symbols of power mentioned in the Mishnah. Hermes often held a staff, Zeus an eagle, and Helios (the sun god) an orb. If they are depicted as having power, the sages feel certain that they are worshiped (and to these images, a sword, crown, and ring are added by the Gemara, 41a). However, if they are not depicted as images of power, then the sages feel one can derive benefit from them without worrying that one is participating in idolatry. Rabban Gamliel believes that any item in the hand of a statue is a symbol of power and is therefore idolatrous. Here, the Mishnah is identifying idolatry as imputing divine power to any entity save God. The worship of power outside a covenantal relationship is idolatrous worship.

These are different questions than those the Mishnah addressed in the first chapter. There, the issue was encountering idolatrous people at an idolatrous time. Here we are dealing with objects that might be idolatrous *sometimes* but aren't being used for that purpose in the present. What guidelines do the sages offer us? If it's something that's clearly used for idolatry, then it is taboo. If the image is not clearly idolatrous, however, then it may be used. The sages aren't xenophobic or obsessed. They're just careful. They don't want to make it impossible for average Jews to live, they just want to separate Jews from idolatry.

### How Much of an Idol Is Idolatrous?

Now, how *much* of an idol is considered an idol? It's as if we were to ask today, "How much radioactivity is a problem and how little may we consider to be merely background radiation?" The answers regarding idolatry depend on how much of the idol is left and how intact the part is. This is almost like the question, "How much of a nuclear missile do you have to destroy for the thing to be considered destroyed?" Is it enough to burn off the rocket or do you have to destroy the silo, too? Or can you merely disassemble the pieces and store them in separate locations? And is it relevant *who* destroys the missile? The sages would answer, "Yes. It's important who destroys it and how much is destroyed."

> **MISHNAH (41a):** If one finds fragments of images, behold they are permitted. If one found a model of a hand or a model of a foot, behold they are prohibited because such objects are worshiped.

> **GEMARA (41b):** It has been stated: If an idol was broken of its own accord, Rabbi Yohanan said that [its fragments] are prohib-

ited. Rabbi Shimon ben Lakish said that they are permitted. Rabbi Yohanan said that they are prohibited because [the idol] has not been annulled. Rabbi Shimon ben Lakish said that they are permitted because [the owner] certainly annuls [the idol] without expressly doing so by saying, "It could not save itself, so how can it save me?"

Let's look at the mishnah first. Fragments of an idol are permitted for use. Today, we might wonder of what possible use fragments might be, but archeology shows us that fragments of monuments were used over and over again as building blocks in different structures. For example, recently, a piece of a victory stele, a commemorative inscribed stone, was discovered that contains the first extra-biblical reference to the house of David ever found. This stele from the First Temple Period (ninth century B.C.E.) was smashed and then the fragments were used as building blocks in a wall built on the pavement at the entrance to the outer gate of the city of Dan.

Now, why is a hand or foot not allowed? Because people who had been healed in a hand or foot would present an image of the healed limb to a god. Alternatively, the Gemara (top of 41b) suggests that an image of a hand or foot is prohibited only when it is placed on a base and is thus worshiped as a representative part of a whole idol.

The Gemara continues by delving into how the fragments were generated. The Gemara, as usual, focuses on inner, human states: intention matters as much as the consequences of physical actions. If the idol simply fell down in a strong wind, Rabbi Yohanan feels that the idol has not been properly annulled. In other words, it is not the destruction of the idol that is sought by the sages but the destruction of *idolatry* within the worshiper. To annul an idol, the idolater must willfully desecrate the statue. Rabbi ben Lakish assumes that even if the idol just fell over, the idolater would annul it, seeing it as powerless.

Reish Lakish's view probably does not take into account how sophisticated a religion idolatry could be. Idolaters did not worship the statues themselves. They were quite aware that the images were human products. The people used the idols to direct their prayers through a powerful visual image.

The sages' view of idolatry may be best expressed in the well-known story of Avram's breaking the idols:

"And Haran died in the presence of his father Terach" (Genesis 11:28). Rabbi Hiyya said: Terach was a manufacturer of idols. One time, he went away someplace and left Avram to sell them in his place.

A man came and wished to buy one. He [Avram] said to him, "How old are you?" He [the man] said to him, "I am fifty or sixty years old." [Avram] said to him, "Woe to such a man who is sixty years old and would worship a day-old object!" [At this] he became ashamed and went.

One time a woman came with a plateful of flour and said to him, "Take this and offer it to them." So he took a stick, broke them [the idols], and put the stick in the hand of the largest. When his father came [back] he said to him, "What have you done to them?" He said, "I cannot conceal it from you. A woman came with a plateful of fine meal and told me to offer it to them. One [idol] said, 'I will eat first,' while another said, 'I will eat first.' The largest among them arose, took the stick and broke them." He said, "Why do you make sport of me? Have they any knowledge?" He [Avram] said, "Do your ears not hear what your mouth is saying?"

Thereupon he seized him and delivered him to Nimrod. [Nimrod] said to him, "Let us worship the fire!"

Avram said, "Let us worship water, which extinguishes fire."

"Then let us worship water!"

"Let us rather worship the clouds, which bear the water."

"Then let us worship the clouds!"

"Let us rather worship the winds, which disperse the clouds."

"Then let us worship the wind!"

"Let us rather worship human beings, who withstand the wind."

He said, "You are just bandying words. We will worship naught but the fire. Behold, I will cast you into it and let the God to whom you bow come and save you from it."

Now Haran [Avram's brother and Lot's father] was standing there undecided. He said [to himself], "If Avram is victorious I will say that I am of Avram's [belief], while if Nimrod is victorious I will say that I am of Nimrod's [belief]." When Avram descended into the fiery furnace and was saved, he [Nimrod]

said to him, "Of whose [belief] are you?" He said, "Of Avram's."
Thereupon he seized him [Haran] and cast him into the fire. His
inwards were scorched and he died in his father Terach's
presence. Hence it is written, "And Haran died in the presence of
his father Terach." [*Bereishit Rabbah* 38:13]

There is a great deal going on in this midrash and it must
be examined piece-by-piece to be appreciated. First of all, what
causes this whole long midrashic explication in the first place? It
is the rather striking statement that Haran died in the presence
of his father. Genesis 11:10–25 outlines how successive generations from the Flood to Avram were born and begot children but
the manner of no one's death is recorded until we reach this
statement that Haran, Avram's brother, died in his father's
presence (Genesis 11:28). The sages therefore feel a need to
explain what is behind the Torah's cryptic statement.

To fully understand Haran's death, the sages set the stage
by giving his family background. It turns out that Avram's
spiritual epiphany and conversion to monotheism caused him to
rebel against his father, Terach. (He isn't Avraham yet. His name
is changed in Genesis 17:5 when he makes a covenant with
God.) Avram's rejection of idolatry is no private business—he
does it with a missionary's zeal. And he takes on progressively
more authoritative individuals. First, he shames the fifty-year-
old man into at least going to another store. Then, he forces his
father to admit that the idols are ineffective as forces in the
world. Finally, he confounds Nimrod the king and withstands
the test of the fiery furnace. In addition, the idolatry that is
defeated is ever-more inward in each part of the story: first, the
idols themselves; second, Nimrod's "reasoning" and worship;
and third, idolatry within the heart that tries to bring an
idolatrous attitude to monotheism.

Avram's brother, Haran, is evidently undecided. He cannot
discern which system is more powerful, his father's idolatry or
his brother's monotheism. He is interested solely in the power
each system musters (a logical thought from an idolater's point
of view). He does not yet understand that monotheism is about
a faithful relationship based on integrity in one's heart. He
makes what is the apparently logical choice: he picks the god

that appears to be most powerful. What he does not understand is that this is not merely one unseen god among deities but *the* God who has no companions or competitors. Not understanding this, he receives no protection from God because he is not participating in the genuine sort of relationship with God that is the hallmark of monotheism. As he is faithless "on the inside," so he is burned "on the inside." It is this moment that the Torah is alluding to when it says that Haran died in Terach's presence.

What a moment of defeat and grief it must have been for Terach! Terach believed in the power of idols and kings. In one day, his son Avram showed him the futility of his way of life and deprived him of two sons, for it is after this that Avram goes to the Land of Israel (Genesis 12:1). What did Terach do? Did he become a believer in Avram's God? Or did he continue to make idols? The text does not suggest a clear answer. We learn that, "Terach died in Charan" (Genesis 11:32). He left his home in Ur of the Chaldeans (Mesopotamia) and traveled to Charan. It is from Charan that Avram leaves for Canaan to found the Jewish religion (Genesis 12:4–5). It is to this town that Jacob flees after he cheats Esau, and it is where his uncle, Lavan, lives (Genesis 27:43, 28:10, 29:4).

This town, Charan, lives up to its name, which means "crossroads." Terach moved from Ur to the "crossroads" but he never completely followed his son's path. It would seem that Charan is a place of soul-searching work where different biblical figures test their true mettle. They know they have succeeded in their spiritual quest when they leave Charan for the Promised Land, as Jacob does after having worked many years for Lavan and learned many lessons in fairness (the hard way!) in Charan. But Terach dies there. Unlike Avram and Jacob, he never makes the commitment to monotheism and dies at the crossroads.

Before we look at Terach too unsympathetically, we should attempt to understand his idolatry. After all, idolatry was an extremely widespread form of faith that lasted for millennia. There must have been *something* in idolatry that drew all those worshipers to it. The sages, through Avram in this midrashic passage, shame the old man and mock Terach by suggesting that it is the idols themselves that were worshiped. As we have already noted, they were foci of prayer, embodiments of forces to which human beings could appeal. The idolater's religious practice was metaphoric in nature. A contemporary poem (Tham 1994) shows how such behavior continues and how it continues to be misinterpreted to this day:

### Ancestor Worship

It's an old story
about an Englishman
visiting his mother's grave
with flowers. He sees a Chinese
woman spreading a feast of roast
chicken, mu shu pork, noodles
before her father's grave.
"When's your father coming out
to eat that food?" he asks.
Smiling, the woman answers,
"Same time your mother
come to smell flowers." [p. 45]

The ethnocentric Englishman in the poem does something we should be careful not to do: assume that our metaphoric actions (bowing before a royal God in prayer, wearing head coverings in that God's presence, etc.) are legitimate while deriding the metaphoric actions of another faith as literalistic and simplistic. The Chinese woman brings the food as an act of devotion, faith, and healing just as the Englishman brings the flowers.

Is this, then, an apology for idolatry? Heaven forbid! But it is essential to understand the environment out of which monotheism developed. Avram had to refute it step by step. This was accomplished most potently in Avram's interaction with Nimrod. First, Avram demonstrates to the king the nonsensical notion of worshiping separate forces in nature. Second, he then demonstrates that the God he worships is above one of the most powerful forces of nature: fire. Finally, through Haran's death, God demonstrates that the idea of worshiping power is, itself, idolatry.

Interestingly, this worship of power is how one of the most

tragic figures in rabbinic literature, Elisha ben Abuya, is led astray. He was a great sage, one of the four seekers who entered the realm of mystical speculation. After he left this "paradise" he apostatized and became an idolater. He attributes his downfall to the very reason that he was brought to Torah: out of a reverence for its power, not out of a love of it.

> [Elisha] said . . . , "[How does one explain the verse] 'The end of a thing is better than its beginning' (Ecclesiastes 7:8)? So long as it is good *from* its beginning.
>
> "And so it happened [to me]. My father, Abuyah, was one of the great people in Jerusalem. When the day of my circumcision came, he invited all the great people of Jerusalem and sat them down in one place, with Rabbi Eliezer and Rabbi Yehoshua in another place. When they had eaten and drunk they began clapping [their hands] and dancing. Rabbi Eliezer said to Rabbi Yehoshua, 'While they are occupying themselves in their way we will occupy ourselves in our way.' And they sat down and engaged in the study of the Torah, from the Torah to the Prophets, and from the Prophets to the Writings. And fire fell from the heavens and surrounded them.
>
> "Abuyah said to them, 'My masters, have you come to burn my house down around me?'
>
> "They said to him, 'God forbid! But we were sitting searching and going over the words of the Torah, from the Torah to the Prophets, and from the Prophets to the Writings, and the words were as bright as when they were given from Sinai. And the fire went about us as it went out from Sinai'. . . .
>
> "Abuyah, my father, said to them, 'My masters, if this is the power of the Torah, if this son of mine lives, I will dedicate this son of mine to Torah.' Because his [original] intention was not pure [lit., for the sake of heaven], therefore it was not realized in the case of this man [Elisha, speaking of himself in the third person]." (*Y. Hagigah* 2:1, 77b, pp. 45–50). *The Talmud of the Land of Israel, Volume 20*, Jacob Neusner, Trans. *Hagigah* and *Moed Qatan*.)

This passage is part of a long dialogue between Rabbi Meir and Elisha ben Abuya. Rabbi Meir was one of the greatest sages who ever lived and was Elisha's disciple even after Elisha forsook Judaism. This conversation takes place on Shabbat.

Elisha is riding on a horse, and Rabbi Meir is walking at his side. (At the end of this conversation, when they have reached the limit of permissible travel on Shabbat, Elisha, who has been counting his horse's footfalls, tells Rabbi Meir to turn back. Rabbi Meir then says, "You, too, turn back!" Their relationship is beautiful and heartbreaking.)

Why did Elisha's learning not inoculate him, as it were, against idolatry? Because his learning came from an idolatrous impulse. His father, an extremely wealthy man, only wanted his son to learn Torah after he realized that Torah learning could be a source of power. Thus, it is no accident that Elisha turned to idolatry. It was the logical outcome of the impulse that brought him to Torah. The worship of power is idolatry. A relationship of honor, respect, devotion, and love in which power has a place—this is Judaism's monotheism.

## How Do You Take Idolatry Out of an Idol?

How does one deal with the image of something that may have been used in idolatrous worship? And what, exactly, is to be considered a part of idolatry? Is every image idolatrous? Or are some images more likely to have been the foci of idolatrous worship than others? The next mishnah addresses these questions?

> MISHNAH (42b): If one finds utensils upon which is the figure of the sun or a figure of the moon or a figure of a dragon, he casts them into the Salt Sea. Rabban Shimon ben Gamliel says: If it is upon precious utensils they are prohibited, but if upon common utensils they are permitted.

Casting something into the Salt Sea means that it cannot be recovered or used again, so the mishnah is mandating that idols be utterly destroyed beyond any hope of recovery. Now, does this mean that your scarf with a picture of a dragon on it or your plates with pictures of the moon on them have to be destroyed? Rabban Gamliel rules that only those items with images that are precious, such as bracelets or signet rings (Gemara, 43b), are likely to have been worshiped. Workaday items such as pots and pans are considered to have merely been decorated. Again, the image is not the problem; the worship of it, the imputing of power to it, is. Idolatrous worship is akin, in the sages' minds, to radioactive contamination: once radioactivity has entered an item, the contamination cannot be neutralized and the item must be disposed of. However, if no contamination has become attached to the item, then it is fit for use. So, if an image has not been worshiped, then it is not contaminated. Again, it is the idolatry, not the idol, that is the problem.

Now, according to the Gemara, there is a way of decontaminating something that has been used for idolatrous purposes so that it may be used again. An idol worshiper must annul the item by treating it as if it has no power. Then the item is considered to be "decontaminated":

GEMARA (43a): Rabbah bar Bar Hanah said in the name of Rabbi Yehoshua ben Levi: One time I was walking after the great Rabbi Elazar Hakkappar along the road and he found a ring and on it was the figure of a dragon. And a child [who was] an idolater passed and he said nothing to him. Then an adult idolater passed and [Rabbi Elazar] said to him, "Annul it" (i.e., treat it disrespectfully or damage it), but he did not annul it. He [Rabbi Elazar] struck him until he annulled it. We learn three things from this. We learn that an idolater can annul an idolatrous object that belongs to himself or to his fellow. We learn that [if the idolater] understands the nature of the idolatrous object and its mode of worship he can annul it, but if he is ignorant of its nature and mode of worship he cannot annul it. We learn that [we may force an idolater] to annul the object against his will.

Rabbi Hanina ridiculed [the foregoing statement, saying]: Does not the great R. Elazar Hakkappar agree with what is taught: If a person rescued something from a lion, bear, leopard, or from a robber, a river, or from what the tide throws up, or the overflow of a river; or if a person finds something in a camp or main highway or in a place where many people congregate, behold the object belongs to him because the owner despairs of recovering it!—Abaye said: Granted that [the owner] despaired of recovering it, but did he despair of its sacred character? He must have said [to himself]: If an idolater finds it he will worship it; if a Jew finds it, since it is a valuable object, he will sell it to an idolater who will worship it.

How do you expel idolatry out of an idol? By having an idolater debase the idol; i.e., treat it as if it has no power. Only an adult, who understands what he is doing, can adequately perform this annulment. Now, we may be surprised and even shocked that the sages permit us to use force to cause an idolater to annul the idol. There is no room, in this passage, for a "live and let live" philosophy. Idolatry is the enemy. It is to be fought at every possible moment. It is not the idols themselves that are the problem but the *idolatry within persons* that repels the sages. This is a remarkable concept. Monotheism is a religion of motivations and relationships. Judaism is not diverted by destroying idols. The sages recognize that what must be changed is the idolater's behavior and inner state. *That* is the crucial matter, not the images themselves.

These nullifications must be accomplished in a thoroughgoing manner. Rabbi Hanina raises an objection to Rabbi Elazar Hakkappar's teaching. The person who lost the dragon ring would certainly have despaired of recovering the object. It is useful to know that in Judaism an object is not lost until the owner has despaired of finding it, another example of how inner states determine reality in the sages' system. For example, let's say you're traveling in another city and you leave your umbrella in a cab. You don't remember the cab number or even the cab company. You don't even think about the umbrella until you leave the airport in your hometown and realize you left the umbrella in the cab. At this point, you will likely give up hope of ever retrieving the umbrella. This umbrella is now *hefker*, ownerless. Note that being ownerless depends on the owner's state of mind. This mental turning point of giving up hope of finding something is called *yei'ush*, despair. The teaching that Rabbi Hanina cites expounds this basic principle. If people lose objects in a busy, public place or have them stolen or lose them because a wild animal carries them off, they immediately despair of recovering the item. The article is then ownerless and any finder can claim it. Thus the dragon ring, lost on an open road, is ownerless property and can be immediately claimed.

However, Abaye points out that Rabbi Elazar Hakkappar's ruling isn't about ownership, it's about idolatry. The owner of this idolatrous ring might despair of ever recovering it, but he would be relatively confident that it would continue to be worshiped as an idol. Either an idol worshiper would find it or a Jew would find it and sell it to an idolater. So the idolater who lost this image would not have annulled the idolatry within it. This is why Rabbi Elazar Hakkappar was right to have the ring's idolatry annulled before he picked it up.

Again, we note that this behavior probably raises modern eyebrows alarmingly. It is difficult to imagine a modern analogy to this ancient situation. The ones that come to mind are not very precise parallels at all. Perhaps one analogy would be if a survivor of a concentration camp made an SS officer tear up or spit on a Nazi flag. The aim is to change the person's viewpoint and to have that change manifested in some concrete, public way. And the opposite is also true: the sages want public, concrete manifestations of a Jew's fealty to God. There are literally hundreds of ways to do this, that is, by doing mitzvot.

## When Imitation *Isn't* Flattery: Rooting Out Idolatry, Not Idols

All this consideration of idolatrous items leads the Gemara to consider the role of images and holy objects in Judaism. How could one prevent people from worshiping these objects as idols, so to speak, by setting up replicas of the Temple all over the world? The sages accomplished this by prohibiting not only the making of God's image but also manufacturing images of the Temple.

GEMARA (43a): A person may not make a house after the design of the Temple, or a porch after the design of the Temple porch, a courtyard after the design of the Temple court, a table after the design of the table [in the Temple], or a candelabrum after the design of its candelabrum. But he may make one with five, six, or eight [branches], but with seven he may not make it even though it be of other metals.

We are forbidden to construct buildings in the image of the Temple. Note how carefully this *baraita* is phrased: three main parts of the Temple—the *heichal* (the sanctuary), the *ulam* (the entrance hall), and the *azarah* (the courtyard)—are explicitly forbidden. Not only are replicas of the Temple's architecture forbidden, but the accouterments of worship are also not to be replicated. A bronze or silver candelabrum may not even be made in the same shape of the Temple's golden menorah because, in times of distress, the menorah in the Temple was made of other metals. Thus, any replication of the Temple cult items is forbidden.

This teaching is many faceted. There was some aspect of competition between the sages and the priesthood while the Temple stood and even for centuries after it was destroyed. The sages and their system of observances were consistently seen as second-best when compared with the Temple and its priesthood. Indeed, this attitude of reverence toward the Temple is enshrined in any number of practices, such as giving *cohanim* (priests) and *levi'im* (Temple singers) the first and second *aliyot* to the Torah and daily prayers for the restoration of the Temple and its cult. So this limitation on imitation of the Temple could be seen as a sign of reverence. However, it also served the political needs of the sages by doing away with constant confrontations with images that would have glorified their "competitors," the priests, and turned these images into idols. It probably served both purposes, although only the former reason was given explicitly for the ruling.

Did people follow the sages' teachings on this topic? Archeological remains of synagogue mosaics show that Jews made detailed replicas of the Temple's accouterments and portrayed images of God at which the sages certainly must have looked askance. For example, in the fifth century C.E. synagogue mosaic of Beit Alpha in Northern Israel, three "screens" depict redemptive scenarios of Judaism. As one enters the synagogue, the first third of the floor shows the binding of Isaac. Abraham holds the knife above Isaac and the altar, fire, ram, and bush are all clearly depicted. In the middle of the floor is the zodiac with the sun riding a chariot in the center. This is meant to show God's rule over all the heavenly bodies. The third "screen," closest to the ark, portrays the Temple: Its ash shovels and censors, shofars, the curtains before the holy of holies, the ark, lulavs, and menorahs. Thus, one would see God's redemptive power in the past (the *Akeidat Yitshak*), in the present (the heavens as represented by the zodiac) and in the future (the Temple which is to be rebuilt) depicted on the synagogue floor. Certainly, the sages would have disapproved of the zodiac and perhaps of the depictions of the Temple. However, as these remains show us, the sages seemed to have had little influence over the Jewish public in this regard.

This is an important point for a Talmud student to grasp. Because Jewish law is derived from rabbinic literature, we tend to think of the sages as great authorities with tremendous power. Indeed, long after their deaths they did come to have this standing. However, when they lived, the sages had but limited authority and had to persuade people of their point of view rather than dictate their opinions to a waiting public.

Another example of this phenomenon is a synagogue that had a statue in it and nobody was troubled by it!

**GEMARA (43b):** Behold in the Synagogue of *Shaf-veyativ* in Nehardea a statue was set up; yet Shmuel's father and Levi entered it and prayed there without worrying about the possibility of suspicion. It is different [where there are] many people [together].

This synagogue was a famous one in Babylonia. It was said that God's presence, the *Shekhinah*, rested within this synagogue. It earned its name from its construction. It was made from stones taken from the destroyed first Temple, which fell (*shaf*) and were settled (*v'yativ*, that is, was built again). In light of our previous teaching, this should already cause us some surprise. If we are not to make replicas of the Temple, how much the more so, it would seem, should we not take actual pieces of the Temple and turn them into a synagogue elsewhere! However, not only was this permitted, but this synagogue was considered a special place wherein to meet God's presence.

So it is all the more shocking to learn that there was a statue in this synagogue! This was probably a bust of the king.

Apparently, Shmuel's father and Levi felt comfortable praying there since many people were present and so no suspicion of idolatry arose in anyone's mind. A similar situation could be found in today's synagogues. Frequently, an Israeli flag and a United States flag are displayed on the *bimah*. When worshipers bow toward the ark during the *Amidah* or for the *Aleinu*, it is clear to everyone present that they are directing their prayers to God and are not bowing to the flags or worshiping them.

Again, we note the consistency and subtlety of the sages' method: they are not fixated on destroying idols. Instead, *idolatry* is what they want to destroy. If the sages invested the idols with too much importance, they would inadvertently buttress a belief in idolatrous systems, and they are far too wise to do that. Inner states are the crucial matters, not outer accouterments. This applies to Judaism as well. The Temple is inside a Jew every time that Jew prays with true intention. It's not the Temple itself that needs to be revered but the relationship with God it fostered.

A story in the Mishnah confirms this underlying theme. First, we note that a story in the Mishnah itself is a rather rare phenomenon. Second, this story, unlike the theoretical dictates we've encountered so far in the Mishnah, shows that the Gemara's concern for internal states was already present, if rarely articulated, in the Mishnaic era. No less a figure than Rabban Gamliel is in the presence of an idol without being troubled by it since it is treated as mere decoration:

MISHNAH (44b): Proclus ben Philosoph asked Rabban Gamliel [a question ] in Acco when he [Rabban Gamliel] was bathing in the bath of Aphrodite. He said to him, "It is written in your Torah, 'and there shall cleave naught of the devoted thing to your hand' (Deuteronomy 13:18); [so] why are you bathing in the bath of Aphrodite?" He [Rabban Gamliel] said to him, "We may not answer [questions relating to Torah] in a bath." When he came out he said to him, "I did not come into her domain, she has come into mine." Nobody says, the bath was made as an adornment for Aphrodite, but he says, Aphrodite was made as an adornment for the bath. Another reason is, if you were given a large sum of money, you would not enter the presence of an idol when polluted by a seminal emission, nor would you urinate before it. But this [statue of Aphrodite] stands by a sewer and all the people urinate before it. [In the Torah] it is only stated, "[you shall utterly destroy . . .] their gods (Deuteronomy 12:2)"—i.e., what is treated as a deity is forbidden, what is not treated as a deity is permitted.

In three ways Rabban Gamliel demonstrates that it is a person's inner relationship to his or her god that is important, not the actual statue itself. This story is set in a bathhouse that apparently had a statue of Aphrodite in it. Public baths were important institutions in the ancient world. The idolater, who either used to be a Jew or has some interest in Judaism since he quotes a Torah verse, asks Rabban Gamliel how he can bathe in such a place. Rabban Gamliel first demonstrates his own reverence for Torah by refusing to answer the question in an inappropriate place. Proclus might quote words of Torah in a place of nakedness and excrement, but Rabban Gamliel will not. This is his first demonstration that one's inner devotion is the crucial matter, not outward appearances. His second is that the bathhouse was built first and the statue was placed in it, perhaps much later, as a decoration and that therefore there can be no suspicion that the whole bathhouse was built as a temple for this idol. This is a logical argument that has nothing to do with theology. However, now Rabban Gamliel turns the idolater's own theology back on him. Even on a bet, Proclus would not come to an idol in a disrespectful way, that is, in a state of ritual impurity or nakedness. The whole problem with idols was that idolaters respected them too much, treated them as if they had power. But people walk before this statue naked and do disrespectful things before it. Clearly, they do not impute any power to this statue. The idolaters themselves consider it a mere decoration. As such, it is not a problem for a Jew to be around this statue. Again, the sages are showing a consistent bent: what is to be rooted out is paganism, not pagan statues themselves.

### What Do You Do with a Feature of Nature That's Been Contaminated with Idolatry?

Up until now, this chapter of the Mishnah has dealt with idols, pieces of idols, and statues that might have been idols.

(The Gemara has, as was seen in previous chapters, focused on idolatry within people.) Now, the Mishnah moves a step further out into the world and considers how Jews should deal with actual features of nature that have been worshiped idolatrously, such as an *asheirah*. The *asheirah* is a somewhat obscure cult figure. As the Torah commands chopping it down and burning it, we may deduce that it was made of wood. It was probably placed near the altar and may have been a sacred pole, a grove of trees, or an image of the goddess *Asheirah*, who was the consort of *Baal*. *Asheirah* was associated with fertility and was called the progenitress of the seventy gods. Idolaters also worshiped hills. Hills and mountains are important in many religions, including Judaism, as one physically ascends and is closer to heaven at the top of a hill or mountain. Altars were erected on the tops of hills for idolatrous worship.

How were Jews to deal with these items of idolatrous worship? It would be economically and physically untenable to call a whole mountain range or set of hills off limits because they were associated with idolatry. This would be especially true in Israel which, except for the coastal plain, is made up of pretty much nothing *but* hills. So the sages, consistent with their previous rulings, prohibit that which has been fashioned by idolatry, but that which God formed is legitimate for use.

> **MISHNAH (45a):** If idolaters worship mountains and hills, these are permitted; but what is upon them is prohibited, as it is said, "You shall not covet the silver or the gold that is on them" (Deuteronomy 7:25). Rabbi Yose HaGallili says: [It is stated, "You shall utterly destroy all the places in which the nations whom you are to dispossess served] their gods upon the high mountains" (Deuteronomy 12:2), not their mountains that are their gods, and their gods upon the hills, not their hills that are their gods.
>
> [But] why is an *asheirah* prohibited? Because there was manual labor connected with it and whatever has manual labor connected with it is prohibited.
>
> Rabbi Akiba said: Let me expound and decide [the interpretation] before you: wherever you find a high mountain or elevated hill or green tree, know that an idolatrous object is there.

The sages are operationalizing the general edict found in Deuteronomy:

> You shall surely destroy all the places, wherein the nations that you are to dispossess served their gods, upon the high mountains, and upon the hills and under every leafy tree. And you shall break down their altars, and dash in pieces their pillars and burn their *asheirim* in fire and you shall hew down the graven images of their gods; and you shall destroy their name out of that place. [Deuteronomy 12:2–3]

It seems clear that the Torah is mandating that one go to idolatrous places, such as mountains, hills, and leafy trees, and destroy the altars, pillars, and *asheirim* that one finds in those places. However, one might also read the text to mean that the places *themselves* should be destroyed. So this mishnah teaches explicitly that the idols are to be destroyed but the places are permitted for Jewish use.

Anything that was shaped by the efforts of human idolatry is to be destroyed. Thus, the pole or wood object that constitutes an *asheirah* is forbidden. Rabbi Akiba understands the apparent redundancy in Deuteronomy 12:2 to indicate that in each one of these places idolatry is practiced. The verse could have stopped by adjuring us to destroy all the places, but it goes on to specifically name three kinds of locales: mountains, hills, and leafy trees. Rabbi Akiba feels that these places are certainly tainted by idolatry since the Torah takes such great pains to name them explicitly.

The Gemara goes even further than the Mishnah. In general, the Mishnah focuses on the concrete: what can be measured, quantified, and objectively observed. The Gemara pushes the limits of this mishnah to their furthest extent by including the following passage in its commentary on the mishnah:

> **GEMARA (46a):** A *tanna* recited [as follows] before Rav Sheshet: If idolaters worship mountains and hills, these are permitted [for Jews to make use of] and their worshipers [should be destroyed] with the sword. [If they worshiped] plants and

herbage, these are prohibited, and their worshipers [should be destroyed] with the sword.

We come back to the refrain of the Gemara regarding idolaters: it is idolatry within the heart that is to be destroyed. *That* is the goal, not the destruction of the idols or the locations wherein they reside. The mountains and hills are permitted to Jews since no human labor has shaped them. The plants, on the other hand, having been tilled by human hands and therefore tainted by idolatry, are forbidden.

The Gemara's theme throughout this chapter of the tractate has been consistent: idolatry is to be destroyed from within. It is people's *souls* that are the focus of the sages' efforts, not the external world, over which they had little control. Here we see in the most explicit terms possible the development of Judaism from the Torah, through the Mishnah and into the Gemara: An ever-inward turning from the world of war and politics to the world of the spirit.

# 4

# Finding Idolatry
# and Holiness Everywhere

If you listen to popular music, you know that one of the components that can really "make" a song is the bass guitar. While the vocalist and keyboard are expounding the melody, the bass provides a constant rhythm that keeps the piece together and moving consistently. The Gemara continues to provide a steady rhythm to the Mishnah's changing melody in this chapter.

In the fourth chapter of this tractate, we see how consistently the Gemara zeros in on peoples' inner states as the locus of idolatry. The Mishnah continues its orderly progression of examining ever-less-central forms of idolatry. In the first chapter the Mishnah looked at idolatrous persons and idolatrous times. In the second chapter, contact with idolatrous persons in everyday life was explored. The third chapter of the Mishnah dealt with idols and pieces thereof. In this, the fourth chapter of the Mishnah, items associated with idols will be dealt with. In particular, the distinction between wine used in idolatrous ceremonies and wine used in Jewish rites is drawn out. This distinction, and the rules that maintain it, will occupy the fifth chapter of the Mishnah as well. Through all this, the Gemara maintains its interest in the inner state of idolatry as the true enemy.

## Wine and Its Meaning in Idolatry and Judaism

If we are to comprehend these last two chapters of tractate *Avodah Zarah*, we must understand the meaning of wine in the

101

idolatrous world and in Judaism. At the outset, the modern reader must be forewarned that what will be described may seem strange and perhaps reminiscent of other faiths. These are important and true insights. There are deep connections between Judaism and idolatry and Judaism and Christianity. Understanding how these faiths are similar also helps us understand how they are different.

How did wine function in idolatrous rites? We will focus on the Greek use of wine in every day rituals. Erwin Goodenough outlines several reasons why Greeks would ritually drink wine (1956, 6:9). For example, they would make private libations (i.e., spilling wine) to their gods before undertaking a dangerous task. They would use wine as a means of atonement and as a way to confirm oaths. They also used wine before, during or after, but always after, meals and at drinking festivals as well as drinking at the graves of the departed. Jews will immediately recognize some parallels: we spill wine from our cups at Havdalah and Pesach. The blessing after meals was said over a cup of wine in ancient days, and this form of the benediction is still preserved in the Passover seder (the third cup of wine) and after festive meals, such as at weddings.

What motivated Greeks to use wine in these ways? The funeral banquets were, in part, a feeding of the gods with wine and the blood wine so closely resembles. The departed souls needed this wine to survive in their life after death. In rites for the living, wine was closely associated with the god Dionysus, the god of ecstasy and fertility. Thus, wine in the ancient world became a symbol of sexuality, fertility, and life eternal. Dionysus was also associated with fire (and its attendant light), which, to the Greeks, was a liquid (Goodenough, 1936, 6:21). By pouring out a libation, "[the] god, with whom one usually shared the cup of the libation, to all appearances shared in the feast, or, more properly, the banqueters drank in company with the god. So originally all drank from a single cup from which the god had first taken his share" (Goodenough 1956, 6:10).

How did these ideas about wine become part of Jewish practice, as they undoubtedly have? Let us first examine the *kiddush* recited on Friday nights and on festivals. The cup of wine is raised to "catch" God's effulgence that overflows like a fountain so that we might imbibe God's very essence through the wine. This is quite reminiscent of a Jewish wedding ceremony, which is not coincidentally called *kiddushin*. The bride and groom solemnize their agreement by imbibing wine from the same cup that, through a benediction, has been infused with God's essence. Thus, God is a partner and witness in this covenant the couple makes. *Kiddush*, then, is a sort of mystical wedding rite between Jews and God, making Shabbat as joyous as a wedding day. Indeed, just as at a wedding, on Shabbat there is a festive meal, with participants dressed in white, singing, and so forth. And wine is a central agent that creates weddings, Shabbatot, and festivals. Wine is the movable, imbibible vehicle that tangibly brings God's essence into everyday life.

This being the case, we can begin to understand the sages' rules regarding wine. If wine was to be used for Jewish consumption, it had to be guarded every moment from idolatrous pollution lest a Jew inadvertently drink wine that had captured the imbibible essence of some pagan god. Such wine was called *yein nesekh*, "libation wine." It would be hard to find such wine today. Wine of gentiles (e.g., Christian Brothers brandy) is called *stam yeinam*, "ordinary wine." Jews are not allowed to drink such wine, although they may sell it as there is no taint of idolatry on it. Today, many Jewish movements demand that kosher wine be used for religious ceremonies but allow nonkosher wine to be consumed at other times. Orthodox Judaism, however, mandates that all wine consumed be kosher.

Like many rules and concepts in Judaism, this set of laws makes sense only if we understand the theology behind it. For example, the Temple sacrifices seem to be the senseless slaughter of innocent animals without an understanding of the role atoning blood plays in Judaism. Likewise, the requirement of physical perfection in the priests is the basest sort of discrimination until one understands that the cult, and all who played a part in it, had to accurately reflect the perfection of the heavenly congregation of angels that gathered when the sacrifices were offered. Any imperfection below would mar the symmetry and make the service inadequate. The rules are intelligible only when the theology behind them, implicitly understood in ancient days, is made explicit to our modern minds.

Though the connection is rarely brought out, the similarities between wine and blood may be important. In the Temple, the three holy fluids were blood (the sacrifices), oil (the menorah), and water (for purification). After the Temple's destruction, and the attendant loss of blood for ritual use, wine may have become the replacement for that holy fluid. Indeed, the wine for the four cups used at the Pesach seder must be a mixture of wine and water (wine was commonly mixed in this way before drinking) that looks like blood, that is, the wine should be red (*B. Pesachim* 108b). This is especially telling since the blood of the Pesach sacrifice played such a central role in this spring rite.

Religious impulses do not disappear because military might destroys institutions. The need for atoning, connecting blood did not vanish when the Temple was destroyed. Rather, it may have taken a new form: wine that could stand in the place of this blood until the messianic era, when the sacrificial rites would be restored. In this context, then, guarding wine from idolatry was as important as guarding the Temple from it, a sort of constant reenactment of the Macabee's Hannukkah story.

Given this background, we may now be able to comprehend the rules laid out in these last two chapters of *Avodah Zarah* regarding wine. Just one more thought may aid our understanding. Unlike idols, wine is ubiquitous, mobile, and fungible. That is, wine could be valid for Jewish consumption or not based on the circumstances of its treatment. Thus, it is an ideal material vehicle through which the sages could explore the spread of idolatry's influence into everyday life.

## How Much Idolatry, How Much Holiness, Is There in a Given Object?

The quantification of spiritual phenomena is one of the Oral Torah's, and particularly the Mishnah's, hallmarks. The Mishnah has a predilection for defining when, how, and how much when discussing spiritual issues. Such an attitude provides a fresh perspective on what is often considered the totally subjective world of spirituality. The Mishnah seems, with all this quantification and measurement, to be saying, "Spirituality can be, and is, rational. Its effects can be measured like precipitation." In the first mishnah of this chapter, the degree to which idolatry penetrates items near an idol is examined:

> **MISHNAH (49b):** Rabbi Yishmael says: If three stones are lying side by side next to a Merkulis, they are prohibited; but if there are two they are permitted. And the sages say: If [the stones] appear to be connected with it, they are prohibited [whatever their number]; but if they do not appear to be connected with it, they are permitted [even if there are more than three stones].

The Mishnah presents a technical problem relating to different forms of idolatry. In *Mishnah Sanhedrin* 7:6, we learn of all sorts of ways one could worship an idol. One might worship the statue itself, bring sacrifices to it, burn incense before it, or declare, "This is my god!" That mishnah then goes on to note the special way a Merkulis is worshiped: by casting stones at it. This Roman god Merkulis (Mercurius) is the Greek god Hermes, who was to benefit travelers. Wayfarers used to erect a pyramid of one stone on top of two others, and anyone who wanted to join this worship threw a stone thither. It is this configuration of three stones (the original "pyramid" next to the Merkulis) that Rabbi Yishmael deems idolatrous. According to his view, only this configuration of stones is idolatrous. Two stones by the idol would merely be two stones. The sages, however, focus on the idea that any stone near an idol may be a piece of that idol and, as such, is obviously forbidden. This delineation of what is associated with an idol and what is not, and how strong this relationship is, has its photo-negative image in the way the sages evaluate accouterments of holiness:

> **MISHNAH:** If the townspeople sell the town square, they may buy with the proceeds a synagogue;
> [if they sell] a synagogue, they may buy [with the proceeds] an ark;
> [if they sell] an ark they may buy wrappings [for scrolls];
> [if they sell] wrappings (26a) they may buy books;
> [if they sell] books they may buy a [Sefer] Torah.

But if they sold a [Sefer] Torah they may not buy [with the proceeds] books:

> if [they sell] books they may not buy wrappings;
> if [they sell] wrappings they may not buy an ark;
> if [they sell] an ark they may not buy a synagogue;
> if [they sell] a synagogue they may not buy a town square.

The same applies to any money left over.

**GEMARA (26b):** Our Rabbis taught [in a *baraita*]: Accessories of a mitzvah may be thrown away. Accessories of holiness are stored away.

The following are accessories of a mitzvah: a sukkah, a *lulav*, a shofar, fringes.

The following are accessories of holiness: sacks [for keeping scrolls] of the Scripture in, tefillin, and mezuzot, a case for a Sefer Torah, and a case for tefillin and tefillin straps. (*Mishnah Megillah* 25b–26a; *B. Megillah* 26b)

Just as there are descending levels of idolatry that the Mishnah is methodically examining in this tractate, from most idolatrous to least idolatrous, so there are ascending levels of holiness associated with items used in Jewish worship. In general, as we see from the mishnah and *baraita* above, the closer something is to actual Torah text, whether it be the entire scroll of the law or the parchments within tefillin and mezuzot, the holier that item is. Items with which we perform mitzvot but that are not in contact with the holy words themselves may be thrown away, such as an old *lulav*. However, the other items (e.g., tefillin cases) must be stored away and may not be disgraced by being placed in the trash. Just as in our mishnah the idol contaminates everything that is used in its service, so Torah spreads holiness to the things with which it is associated.

When we contrast these two mishnahs, we begin to develop a sense of the sages' view of the world, at least as expressed in the Mishnah. The Mishnah systematically tried to qualify and objectify the most ethereal emotional and spiritual phenomena, such as idolatry and monotheism. The Mishnah takes these theologies and associates them with concrete objects to different degrees in order to show, operationally, how these theologies function in the world.

## The Secret of Idolatry

There is an obvious danger in the sages' expressing too much loathing and abhorrence of idols. Their intense ire may, inadvertently, buttress the belief that the idols have some sort of power. Therefore, the Gemara takes pains to make it clear that it is the *worship* of idols that is the problem, not the idols themselves, although they are to be avoided *because* of the spiritual energy erroneously lavished on them.

GEMARA (52a): [We understand] Rabbi Akiba's reason for the view that the idol of an idolater is immediately forbidden, but whence [does he derive that the idol] of a Jew [is not forbidden] until it is worshiped?—Rav Yehudah said: Scripture [says], "And sets it up in secret" (Deuteronomy 27:15), [i.e., he is not involved in the curse] until he performs towards it things that are done in secret (cf. Deuteronomy 13:7).

And how does the one [i.e., Rabbi Yishmael, explain this phrase]?—He requires it in accordance with the teaching of Rabbi Yitshak, for Rabbi Yitshak said: From whence [do we know that] an idol belonging to a Jew must be removed out of sight? As it is said, "And sets it up in secret" (Deuteronomy 27:15).

[And from where does] the other [i.e., Rabbi Akiba, derive this regulation]? He deduces it from what Rav Hisda said in the name of Rav: whence [do we derive that the idol] of a Jew [is not forbidden] until it is worshiped? As it is said, "You shall not plant you an *asheirah* of any kind of tree beside the altar" (Deuteronomy 16:21)—as an altar must be removed out of sight, so an *asheirah* [belonging to a Jew] must be removed out of sight.

And what does the one [i.e., Rabbi Yishmael, make of this verse]?—He requires it in accordance with the teaching of Rabbi Shimon ben Lakish, who said: Whoever appoints an unworthy judge is as though he plants an *asheirah* in Israel, as it is said, "Judges and officers shall you make you in all your gates" (Deuteronomy 16:18), and near it [is written], "You shall not plant you an *asheirah* of any kind of tree" (Deuteronomy 16:21). Rav Ashi said: [Should he have appointed such a judge] in a place where there are disciples of the Sages, it is as though he had planted an *asheirah* by the side of the altar, as it is stated, "Beside the altar" (cf. *Sanhedrin* 7b).

Rabbi Akiba rules that an idol is abhorrent from the moment an idolater completes its manufacture because it leads to an abomination, idol worship. Note, again, that the idol isn't the problem, as it is merely a statue. It is the use to which the idol is put that is problematic. We have here a dispute between two great rivals: Rabbi Akiba and Rabbi Ishmael. Rabbi Akiba favored rather fanciful interpretations of Torah, while Rabbi Ishmael insisted on a closer reading.

To truly elucidate this issue, the sages posit the case of a Jew who has an idol. In this situation, it is possible to ask, "When, exactly, does the statue become an idol?" It is the worship of the idol that makes it abominable. And it is irrelevant whether this worship takes place in private or in public. The Torah itself makes this clear:

> Cursed be the man that makes any carved or molten idol, an abomination to the Lord, the work of the hands of a craftsman, and sets it up in *secret (basater)*. [Deuteronomy 27:15]
>
> If your brother, the son of your mother, or your son, or your daughter, or the wife of your bosom, or your friend who is as your own soul, entice you *secretly (baseter)* saying, Let us go and serve other gods, which you have not known, you nor your fathers; of the gods of the peoples who are round about you, either near to you, or far off from you, from one end of the earth even to the other end of the earth, you shall not consent to him, nor hearken to him; nor shall your eye pity him, nor shall you spare, nor shall you conceal him, but you shall surely kill him. [Deuteronomy 13:7–10]

Idolatry was so easy! It was everywhere. You could burn an incense offering to some god on your rooftop, just as your neighbors were doing, and still go to the Temple and offer sacrifices to God. Therefore, the Torah commands that mere public allegiance to God will not suffice. The commitment must be total and absolute. In this, there is no distinction between public and private actions. (Compare this, however, to the distinctions made in the case of Dama in Chapter Two. There's always a balance to be maintained.)

This passage of Gemara comments on various meanings ascribed to this concept of "in secret." After all, this word is not, strictly speaking, necessary. So it must be there to teach us something. What could that something be? There are four possibilities:

1. Setting it up in secret (Deuteronomy 27:15) means worshiping it, which a Jew would only permit himself to do in secret since it's so shameful.

2. Another interpretation of this verse is that a Jew may only possess an idol that is put out of sight. Even if the Jew does not worship the statue, it may not be displayed prominently, lest it give the wrong impression.

3. This interpretation is linked to the idea that just as an altar must be removed, so must an *asheirah* be removed (Deuteronomy 16:21). Since these things must be removed, the sages extend the verse to mean that any idol must be removed from sight.

4. Finally, the Gemara makes it plain that idol worship = the perversion of justice through the worship of power by equating it with the appointment of unworthy judges. How in the world do the sages make such a leap? To the sages, nothing in the Torah is haphazard. If two verses are placed together, it is done in order to teach something. Thus, they derive this lesson from these verses in Deuteronomy.

> Judges and officers shall you make you in all your gates, which the Lord your God gives you throughout your tribes: and they shall judge the people with righteous judgment. You shall not wrest judgment; you shall not respect persons, neither take a bribe for a bribe blinds the eyes of the wise and perverts the words of the righteous. Justice, only justice shall you pursue that you may live and inherit the land which the Lord your God gives you. You shall not plant you an *asheirah* of any tree near the altar of the Lord your God, which you shall make you. Neither shall you set you up any pillar; which the Lord your God hates. [Deuteronomy 16:18–21]

The sages feel there must be a reason the verses about justice and the prohibition against idolatry are placed next to each other. The message the sages derive from this arrangement is that failing to set up a righteous justice system is as bad as idolatry. The sages, and the fair judges who come from their ranks, are equated with the altar because they both provide the path to repentance and atonement for sin. Dishonest judges, who are in it for the power, are like idols planted next to God's altar. Faithless judges poison the very system they are supposed to maintain.

This piece of Gemara moves from condemning worship of an idol, to barring the displaying of an idol that is not worshiped, to the removing of such an idol, and, finally, to the metaphoric extension of idolatry that is then considered off-limits. In this way, the Gemara "pushes the envelope" of the boundaries that keep idolatry out of Judaism. It moves from the worship of idols to explicitly identifying idolatry with the perversion of power. This is a classic example of how the Gemara can take the Mishnah's concrete agenda and go to the very spiritual core of its essence.

Such an exercise is not merely an idle intellectual one. Rather, it provides a model for metaphorical extension and deep analysis today. If idolatry remains the worship of power and the perversion of justice, how, today, are we allowing idolatry into our lives? How could we be as persistent as the Gemara's sages in identifying it and rooting it out? How can we root it out in ourselves? What secret corner of ourselves are we preserving for our own particular brand of idolatry? What "idol," what myth about money or power, do we secretly hold in our hearts? When will we cleanse that inner altar?

## Why Doesn't God Make It Easy?

"So," one could easily ask oneself, "why doesn't God make it easy? Why doesn't God do away with free will or destroy all the idols and the idol worshipers? That's certainly within God's power. If God hates idolatry so much, why doesn't God make idolatry disappear?" The sages, too, wondered about this issue.

In fact, it was so important that they highlighted their solution by placing it in the Mishnah, a rare example of a story in a literary genre devoted to what might be called legal poetry.

> **MISHNAH (54b):** The Elders [Rabban Gamliel, Rabbi Elazar ben Azariah, Rabbi Yehoshua ben Hananiah, and Rabbi Akiba, in 95 C.E.] in Rome were asked, "If [your God] does not want idolatry, why does He not abolish it?" They said [to the Romans], "If it were something unnecessary to the world that were worshiped, He would abolish it. But people worship the sun, moon, stars, and planets. Should He destroy His universe on account of fools?"
>
> They said [to the Elders], "If so, He should destroy what is unnecessary for the world and leave what is necessary for the world!" They said to them [the Romans], "[If He did that], we should merely be strengthening the hands of the worshipers of these [the essential things that God spared], because they would say, 'Know that these are [surely] dieties, for behold they have not been abolished!'"

If the Jewish God were powerful, then why didn't that God display power? That's what the idolaters want to know. They seem incapable of framing their theological questions in any way save the worship of power. The sages answer that God can't destroy creation just because some people appreciate it in perverted ways. This is a subtle dig at the capriciousness of idolatrous gods. A person could make an offering to one of these gods, and that god might or might not grant the request that accompanied the offering. However, God's relationship with Israel and the world is one of faithfulness and reciprocity. God promised not to destroy creation again no matter how badly humans misbehaved (Genesis 8:21). In this sense, God, while omnipotent, has agreed to let a covenant made with Noah limit Divine power.

Then why, ask the idolaters, doesn't God destroy idols? They understand, apparently, why God does not do away with the heavenly bodies, but God could certainly destroy a few idols! But then, argue the sages, people would worship the heavenly bodies all the more as separate deities since they would not have been destroyed. Idolaters would think that the preservation of the sun and the moon was not because they were necessary for humanity but because they had some power of their own, separate from God, that saved them.

God, according to the sages, has no choice in this matter. Having agreed that the world would not be destroyed, God would become like a pagan deity if God broke a sacred covenant. God's rule would then be about power rather than faithfulness, and that's a losing proposition in monotheism. God has set certain laws of nature in motion, and, barring the miraculous, they are not set aside simply to impress people who already seem misguided and liable to misunderstand demonstrations of power.

The Gemara now goes on to explore why God doesn't do the "logical" thing and destroy idolatry by focusing on that power that was most sought after in the ancient world: the power of fertility. When we think of fertility, we think of sexuality and conception, and certainly this was a focus in the ancient world as well. However, we ought to broaden our understanding of fertility to include not only conception but the sustaining of life. In a world where disease could carry off human beings and one violent storm or swarm of pests might destroy a crop in a day, life was a tenuous affair to start and to maintain. The power to create and maintain life was God's highest gift to humanity. The sages link sexual and theological faithfulness together in this passage:

> **GEMARA (54b):** Our Rabbis taught: Philosophers asked the elders in Rome, "If your God has no desire for idolatry, why does He not abolish it?" They [the sages] said to them, "If it were something of which the world has no need that were worshiped, He would abolish it. But people worship the sun, moon, stars, and planets. Should He destroy the Universe on account of fools? The world pursues its natural course, and the fools who act wrongly will have to render an account [for their actions] in the future.
>
> Another illustration: Suppose a man stole a measure of wheat and went and sowed it in the ground. It is right that it should not grow, but the world pursues its natural course, and the fools who

act wrongly will have to render an account [for their actions] in the future.

Another illustration: Suppose a man has intercourse with his neighbor's wife. It is right that she should not conceive. But the world pursues its natural course, and the fools who act wrongly will have to render an account [for their actions] in the future."

These midrashim are also found in *Mekhilta Bachodesh* 6 on Exodus 20:5 (the midrash on Exodus). There, this passage explains the verse:

You shall not bow down to them nor serve them for I the Lord your God am a jealous God, punishing the iniquity of the fathers upon the children unto the third and fourth generation of those that hate me, but showing mercy to thousands of generations of those that love me and keep My commandments. [Exodus 20:5]

This verse would form a natural background for these stories: if God is so jealous why doesn't God just destroy idolatry and/or idols? God is represented in this Torah verse (part of the Ten Commandments) as a Deity of power. What the idolaters miss is that it is power *in a relationship*, not power alone, that characterizes the God of the Torah.

This passage has three levels, all of which appeal to the "natural course" of the world as the reason God does not destroy idolatry. First, it establishes that the natural course of the world is necessary. Then, it likens idolatry to stealing and finally to adultery. God set up a system, a "natural course" of the world, part of which is free will for humanity. If human beings use that free will to make mistakes or commit sins, it does not nullify the integrity of the rest of the system. God is faithful even when human beings are not. This might give some who do not understand, such as the philosophers, the impression that God is not powerful enough to stop idolatry. Note, again, the idolaters' focus on power. But the Jewish God is a Deity for whom faithfulness and consistency is more important than a show of power.

This passage reflects the basic idea that worshiping other

gods is like adultery. This concept is seen numerous times in the Torah. For example, after the sin of the golden calf (Exodus 32:20), Moses burns the idol, grinds it up, and makes the Israelites drink it. This ritual is extremely similar to the *sotah* rite for a suspected adulterous wife (Numbers 5:11–31). The worship of other gods is as serious a breach of trust as the breaking of the wedding contract. God is often characterized as a groom, Israel as the bride, and the Torah as a wedding contract (*ketubah*). *Mekilta* draws out this parallel explicitly:

> How were the Ten Commandments arranged? Five on the one table and five on the other . . . [On the one tablet] was written: "You shall have [no other god]" (Exodus 20:3). And opposite it on the other tablet was written: "You shall not commit adultery" (Exodus 20:13). Scripture [thus] tells [you] that if one worships idols it is accounted to him as though he committed adultery, breaking his covenant with God. (Bachodesh 8, Mekilta, Volume 2, JPS, pp. 262–263)

If the model of relationship with God is the marital bond, then the finest product of that relationship is fertility: life. So the idolaters in our Gemara passage wonder why God does not deny this desirable outcome to idolaters, who are likened to adulterers, and the sages respond with their parable. Sometimes human sexuality is expressed inappropriately yet it nonetheless has a positive outcome.

It was not only idolaters who wondered why God did not destroy idolatry. Jews, themselves, wondered why God did not annihilate the detested practices. The sages answered these Jews in much the same way that they answered the idolaters: God is more faithful than human beings and will not besmirch Divine honor by being capricious. In this next passage, Zonin, Rabban Gamliel's deputy in the Academy at Yavneh, certainly a knowledgeable, involved Jew (see *B. Baba Batra* 164b and *B. Pesachim* 49a), shows that even Jews of his caliber were puzzled by God's inaction against idolatry:

**GEMARA (55a):** Zonin said to Rabbi Akiba: "We both know in our hearts that there is no reality in an idol. But we see men enter

[the shrine] crippled and come out cured. What is the reason?"
He [Rabbi Akiba] said to him, "I will give you a parable: To what
is the matter like? To a trustworthy man in a city, and all his
townsmen used to deposit [their money] in his charge without witnesses. One person, however, came and deposited [his
money] in his charge with witnesses. One time he forgot and
made his deposit without witnesses. The wife [of the trustworthy
man] said to [her husband], 'Come, let us deny it.' He said to her,
'Because this fool acted in an unworthy manner, shall I destroy
my [reputation for] trustworthiness!'

"It is similar with afflictions. At the time they are sent upon a
person the oath is imposed upon them, 'You shall not come upon
him except on such and such a day, nor depart from him except
on such and such a day, and at such an hour, and through the
medium of so and so, and through such and such a remedy.'
When the time arrives for them to depart, the man [may happen
to] go to an idolatrous shrine. The afflictions say, 'It is right that
we should not leave him and depart. But because this fool acts in
an unworthy way shall we break our oath?' "

Even though Zonin knows idolatry has no power, the
evidence of his eyes seems to suggest that idolatry could be
efficacious. Rabbi Akiba appeals to the idea that has already
been brought forth repeatedly. God is trustworthy. God is
faithful. God expresses power *in a relationship* and will not be
swayed from Divine steadfastness because of humanity's foolishness.

The parable here is easy to understand. Because the man
(God) is so trustworthy, people can leave their money with him
without witnesses. The distrustful man (the idolater) leaves the
money with the man (God) in the presence of witnesses. Note,
again, that the hallmark of idolatry is a lack of relationship based
on mutual trust and responsibility. One time, however, the man
acts in a manner that leaves him vulnerable. The wife (here,
Zonin and Jews like him, who would urge God to destroy
idolatry) urges that the man take the money. However, the man
(God) prizes consistency and honesty more than teaching one
fool a lesson. Table 4–1 may help to draw out the parallels.

**Table 4-1**

| 1st Parable | Explanation | 2nd Parable |
|---|---|---|
| man | God | afflictions |
| untrusting man | idolater | man with afflictions |
| wife | Zonin | Zonin/doubting Jews |

The Gemara draws out the lesson. Afflictions, in this passage, are not capricious horrors but experiences that have a fixed course and that express God's faithfulness. There is a natural order to what God does, and the foolishness of human beings cannot change it even though it appears to be to God's disadvantage that the idolaters not be punished.

This passage points to a very important spiritual truth: there is an order and meaning to God's world, much of which is hidden from human view. The universe is the product of the infinite mind. Our minds are finite. We can never know the fullness of God's plan and creation. Thus, it appears from our human point of view that unjust things are happening. To human beings, afflictions appear capricious. Evil (here, idolatry) goes unpunished. Things don't make sense. God occasionally, from this perspective, does not seem faithful. These passages consistently point out that even people who cultivate a faithful, consistent relationship with God cannot know everything in God's mind. When we try to impose our intellectual rules on God's intellect, we distort out understanding. Only when we begin with the premise that we cannot understand everything and that we will accept that pieces of the puzzle will appear contradictory can we begin to grasp the vastness of God's reality. Coming even to the edge of such understanding makes God's consistency and mercy all the more awe-inspiring.

### How Assimilated Were Jews in the Sages' Days?

The Gemara now turns its attention to the issue of wine possibly tainted by idolatry, as described at the beginning of this chapter. Wine, a ubiquitous, moveable substance was an ideal concrete vehicle for exploring the ways Jews and non-Jews interacted with each other. Our first example may remind some readers of the famous episode of "I Love Lucy" in which she is in a vat stomping on some grapes. In this passage, a Jew and an idolater are in the vat together.

> **GEMARA (56b):** It happened in Nehardea that a Jew and a heathen pressed out wine together. [On the question being put to him as to how this wine was to be considered,] Shmuel delayed three Festivals [before replying].

Nehardea was home to Jews as early as the sixth century B.C.E. and boasted one of Babylonia's most famous yeshivahs. However, the city lay near the border between the Roman and Persian Empires and suffered for it. It was destroyed in 259 C.E. and its yeshivah was moved to the Babylonian cities of Mehoza and Pumbedita. So, when we learn that a Jew and an idolater are pressing wine together in Nehardea, it is something like the equivalent of them doing so in New York City. In other words, this is not a place of ignorant Jews or a small population thereof. Rather, this is behavior being carried on right in the heart of the exilic Jewish community.

Now, the idolater had touched this wine with his feet, not with his hands. This passage is part of a long discussion of idolaters touching Jewish wine and the complexity and difficulty of deciding what to do about such contact. Is such wine only forbidden for Jewish consumption? May it be sold to idol-worshipers? Or is no use to be made of it whatsoever? Shmuel delays answering this question for three festivals. This appears to be a standard way of saying that this is a difficult question that must be settled at periodic gatherings of sages at which more than one expert can be consulted (see *B. Yebamot* 122a, *B. Hullin* 48a, 77a). The actual issue at hand is not critical for us. Indeed, it remains undecided in the Talmud. What is interesting for our purposes is that such a situation could ever occur. It proves, once again, how important it is to look at the sources we have in hand to gain an understanding of our ancestors' lives. With that understanding, we may gain some insight into how to live our own lives.

The major ruling about how wine can become *nesekh* is, quite predictably, based on the internal state of the idolater.

> **GEMARA (57a):** As for their wine, adults render it *nesekh* [by contact with it], but minors do not render it *nesekh*. The following are adults and minors: Adults are those who understand the nature of an idol and how to handle it. Minors do not understand the nature of an idol and how to handle it.

Here, the sages make their theme explicit: idolatry is not about idols. Idolatry is a belief within a person that changes that person's relationship with God and with the world. Someone who can understand what an idol is, and how wine could be used to worship that idol, is someone about whom Jews must be careful with regard to their wine. The curious touch of a toddler from an idolatrous household carries no weight whatsoever. It is only when intention is present that the actions have any meaning. The inner state is always the key for the Gemara.

This is not only the case for idolatry. It is true for the practice of Judaism as well. It is one's inner state that determines one's participation. For example, two boys who, according to formal rules of Jewish etiquette, should not have been able to participate in the invitation to make the blessing after meals (called *zimmun*) are allowed to do so because their inner state shows a maturity beyond their physical state.

> A boy [younger than 13 years old] who knows to whom the benediction is addressed (i.e., God) may be counted for *zimmun*. Abaye and Rava [when they were boys] were once sitting before Rabbah. Said Rabbah to them, "To whom do we address the benedictions?"
> They replied, "To the All Merciful."
> "And where does the All Merciful abide?" Rava pointed to the roof; Abaye went outside and pointed to the sky.
> Said Rabbah to them, "Both of you will become Rabbis."
> This accords with the popular saying, "Every pumpkin can be told from its stalk." [B. *Berachot* 48a]

Inner states are one of the biggest, if not the ultimate, factors in determining what any concrete action means. A grown person who does not understand what the blessing after meals really means can't say it effectively, while a child who does understand can do so. Similarly, a grown idol-worshiper is one against whom precautions must be taken. Inner states are the key.

This chapter of the tractate yields one of the most remarkable examples of assimilation by Jews in the sages' era. We think of intermarriage and laxity in observing the laws of *kashrut* as twentieth century problems. That is far from the case! Here we see that Jews, then too, intermarried:

> GEMARA (59a): Rabbi Hiyya bar Abba once visited Gavla and there saw Jewish women who were pregnant by idolaters who had been circumcised but not immersed [in the *mikveh* to complete their conversion]. He saw wine, which had been mixed by idolaters, being drunk by Jews and lupins eaten when cooked by idolaters. But he said nothing to them.
>
> When he came before Rabbi Yohanan [and reported the matter to him] he [Rabbi Yohanan] said to him, "Go and announce that their children are illegitimate, their wine is *nesekh*, and their lupins [are prohibited] as something cooked by idolaters, because [the inhabitants of Gavla] are not people of Torah (*b'nei Torah*)!

Let's take this passage one bit at a time. The act of conversion to Judaism by men consists of two steps. First the man is circumcised and after the wound has healed, he ritually bathes in the *mikveh* and is then considered a Jew. These women were pregnant by men who had been circumcised but who had not been to the *mikveh* and the men were, thus, in a state of liminality in terms of their Jewish identity. Clearly, their wounds had healed enough that they could have sexual intercourse and impregnate women, so going to the *mikveh* should not have been delayed in their cases. Second, their wine is considered *nesekh*, not because it has necessarily been touched by idolatry but because this community's observances are so lax that the sages want to inculcate in them the idea that one should make a fence around the Torah and distance oneself from anything remotely connected with idolatry. Third, the lupins (beans) would not ordinarily be considered a problematic food, again, except that this community's observances are so negligible that the sages felt the need to bolster communal limits.

In the end, the passage reveals that it is one's inner state, not one's outer actions, that are the most potent determinant of permissibility. "People of Torah" could eat such lupins because they would understand the rules and value the relationship with God from which such rules flowed. The people of the town, however, are clearly indifferent to this relationship with God, and it is for this reason that they are treated strictly.

Relationships. Inner states. The Gemara's beat goes on.

---  5 ---

# How Responsible
# Are Jews for Idol Worship
# in Idolaters?

In the second half of Chapter Four, the Mishnah begins talking about the manufacturing process of *yein nesekh*. In Chapter Five, the Mishnah broadens its scope of inquiry to examine issues connected with *yein nesekh* after its manufacture is completed: storing wine, selling it, spilling it, and so forth. One wonders why Chapter Four of the Mishnah does not end with mishnah 4:7, the story of the philosopher and Rabban Gamliel, which beautifully caps off the whole chapter up to that point and, indeed, the whole tractate. In fact, this whole last chapter-and-a-half of the Mishnah might well have gone into some other order of the Mishnah, such as that of Agriculture or even, owing to the very last mishnah in Chapter Five, Purities. However, the compilers of the Mishnah make a point by assigning these issues about idolaters' wine to *this* tractate. While the laws of tithes and not mixing kinds of produce are important agricultural laws, wine represents something beyond these categories of agriculture. It is a special product that has rich layers of meaning. By placing this material here, the Mishnah shows that it categorizes wine as a theological substance, as it were, more than as an agricultural one.

The Mishnah of Chapter Five explores the way idolatry seeps into Jewish life, quite literally, in the form of *yein nesekh*. The Gemara of this chapter continues its back-beat: relationships and inner states are crucial. In this chapter, the Gemara specifically examines the tiny, everyday moments when Judaism in people comes into contact with idolatry in people. This contrast between Mishnah and Gemara in the tractate's final chapter is at its most pronounced.

### Idolatry, Money, and Living in the World

The first mishnah in this chapter uses *yein nesekh* as a way of objectifying the working relationship between Jews and non-Jews, which may involve the Jew aiding idolatry in some way:

> MISHNAH (62a): If [an idolater] hires [a Jewish] workman to assist him with [transporting] *yein nesekh*, his wage is prohibited. If he hired him to assist him in another kind of work, even if [the employer] said to him, "Move a cask of *yein nesekh* from this place to that for me," this wage is permitted. If he hired [a Jew's] ass to carry *yein nesekh*, its hire is prohibited. [But if] he hired it to sit upon, even if the idolater rested his jar [of *yein nesekh*] upon it, its hire is permitted.

We have already encountered (in Chapter Two) the idea that something done with foreknowledge is different from an accomplished fact (*l'hatkhilah* and *b'd'avad*). This is somewhat similar. If one's relationship is based on work acceptable to a Jew, then if, in the course of that work, the idolater asked something inappropriate, it is permitted for the Jew to honor the request in order to sustain the relationship. However, a Jew is not allowed to take a job *knowing* that it will entail the furtherance of idolatry.

We may wonder, once more, at the world this mishnah presumes to exist, a world in which Jew and idolater work closely together with, one suspects, some mutual sensitivity and knowledge about the other's beliefs. The Mishnah is consistent, as it has been from the beginning of this tractate. It seeks to minimize a Jew's contribution to idolatry, whether that be through limiting trade with idolaters for three days before an idolatrous festival but not prohibiting trade altogether, or by allowing a Jew and an idolater to work together but limiting the Jew's furtherance of idolatry within that relationship. We also note that outer forms are the key to the Mishnah's system: the verbalized agreement and the money exchanged are the measure of the situation.

The Gemara considers a different issue. The mishnah wonders if a Jew may earn money by dealing with idolatry. The Gemara wonders if idolaters may make payment to Jews with money made from the sale of idolatrous goods. This is a slightly more nuanced problem. After all, not only is the Jew not furthering idolatry, as was the case with the mishnah's Jew moving *yein nesekh* around, but having an idolater sell an idol to pay a debt is, in some ways, a diminution of idolatry in the world, which is a good thing. Not surprisingly, the Gemara focuses on one's inner state as it relates to paganism and money:

> **GEMARA (64a):** Again [Rav Nahman, Ulla, and Abimi bar Papi, and Rabbi Hiyya bar Ammi] were sitting together when the question was raised: How is it with the price of an idol in the possession of an idolater? Does [the prohibition] affect the money that is in the possession of an idolater or not?—Rav Nahman said to them: The more probable view is that the price of an idol in the possession of an idolater is permitted, [as may be seen from the incident where some would-be proselytes] came before Rabbah bar Abbahu, and he said to them, "Go and sell all your possessions and then come to be converted." What was his reason? Was it not because he held that the price of an idol in the possession of an idolater is permitted! But perhaps it is different in this later circumstance, because having the intention of becoming a proselyte, each of them must surely have annulled [his idolatrous objects]!—Rather may [support for Rav Nahman's view be obtained] from this teaching (*T. Avodah Zarah* 7:16): If a Jew has a claim for a sum against an idolater and the latter sold an idol or *yein nesekh* and brought him the proceeds, [the money] is permitted to him. But if [the idolater] said to him [the Jew], "Wait until I sell an idol or *yein nesekh* and I will bring you the proceeds," it is prohibited.

This passage is a bit complicated. The four sages are sitting discussing questions of how one should relate to non-Jews. They seem to agree that an idolater's money may be accepted by Jews. The case of the converts is taken as proof of this but is then rejected, for certainly an idolater converting to Judaism would have annulled the idols and therefore this money is not actually money coming from idolatry. So how can Rav Nahman rule that a Jew may accept an idolater's money even if it comes from the sale of idols or *yein nesekh*? Because there is a passage from *Tosefta* (*T. Avodah Zarah* 7:16) that states that one may accept payment from an idolater after he sold an idol or *yein nesekh* to raise the money, however one may not accept the money *l'hatkhilah*, knowing that it will have the taint of idolatry upon it.

The sages seem to be walking an extremely fine line here. They want to keep Jews separate from the taint of idolatry, and yet they also want to make it possible for them to function economically in the world around them. Analogous economic issues are raised in our times. For example, let's say you like a certain brand of sport shoe. You buy them until you learn that they are manufactured in sweat shops in the Far East where children are mistreated. Would you buy the shoes once you know this fact? Or would you buy hand-tied oriental rugs knowing that six-year-old children in India were chained to their work stations to make those rugs? There is a dimension of morality and spirituality connected with economic transactions that the sages recognize. It is almost impossible to make sure that every item you buy or all the money you receive has a perfect ethical and monotheistic pedigree. Nonetheless, when irrefutable information is transmitted to the consumer affirming that some sin is attached to money or goods, the sages seem to be saying that it is a Jew's responsibility to recognize the goods as tainted. The converse is probably true, as well. One may receive added benefit from goods produced for charity or that have a "righteous" pedigree. For example, one may enjoy wearing a "house pin" because it is beautiful *and* take additional pleasure in knowing that it also represents a donation to charities for homeless persons.

### How Can a Non-Jew Be Connected to the Jewish Community?

It is relatively easy to identify what a Jew should do with regard to an idolatrous non-Jew. That, after all, is what this whole tractate is about. But what about the non-Jew who is sympathetic to Judaism? How should such a person be treated by the Jewish community? That is what our next passage outlines:

> GEMARA (64b): Who is a *ger toshav?* Any [Gentile] who takes upon himself in the presence of three *chaveirim* not to worship idols. [These are the] words of Rabbi Meir. But the sages say: Any [Gentile] who takes upon himself the seven commandments that the sons of Noah took upon themselves. Others say: These do not come within the category of a *ger toshav*. But who [then] is a *ger toshav?* A proselyte who eats of animals not ritually slaughtered (*n'veilot*), i.e., he took upon himself to observe all the precepts mentioned in the Torah apart from the prohibition of [eating the flesh of] animals not ritually slaughtered.

A *ger toshav* is, literally, "a resident alien" who lives in Israel and accepts some mitzvot. As we can see from this passage, it is not clear what a person must do to be considered a *ger toshav*. Some think it is merely the formal renunciation of idolatry; some that he must do almost all the mitzvot although he may eat nonkosher food. The middle opinion is that this person must observe the seven laws given to Noah. Before there were Jews, there were still laws that God gave to humanity and that every person, Jew or non-Jew, was bound to follow:

> Concerning seven religious requirements were the children of Noah admonished: setting up courts of justice, idolatry, blasphemy, adultery, and incest, bloodshed and thievery. . . . [Also, against eating] the limb cut from a living beast. . . . [Some also add the prohibitions against] castration . . . and witchcraft. [*Tosefta Avodah Zarah* 8:4–6 //B. *Sanhedrin* 56a–b]

One imagines that a *ger toshav* would have to do more than give up idolatry since this is included in the seven Noachide commandments that apply to everyone. And if a *ger toshav* were to observe everything except the laws of *n'veilah*—eating the carcasses of animals that died of natural causes or that were improperly slaughtered—the *ger toshav* would be more observant than many Jews! So the middle view, in this case, is the one that is accepted. This, by now, should seem odd since it is normally the last view in a passage that is authoritative. Perhaps when this passage was composed there was no definitive decision as to what the *ger toshav* had to do to gain his or her status and so the opinions were simply arranged from most lenient to least lenient.

Perhaps different communities in Israel had different customs regarding the role of non-Jews in their midst. As we have already seen, there was a differentiation between the *chaveir*, who was punctilious about ritual purity and "agricultural taxes" (tithes and so forth) and the *am ha'arets*, who was not careful about these observances. Now we see that non-Jews are also divided into groups. There is the *ger toshav* who has a special status within the Jewish world: a sympathizer and supporter, a fellow traveler. This non-Jew is contrasted with the *oveid kochavim*, the idol-worshiper, and the *min*, the Jew who has become a heretic. It's all a matter of degrees. The *ger toshav* was not, of course, considered a Jew. Yet the *ger toshav* was also not deemed an idolater. This differentiation is consistent with the sages' system emphasizing internal states. It is not a non-Jew's ethnic identity which determines his or her place in the Jewish world but rather the non-Jew's rejection of idolatry and acceptance of Judaism which determines that person's status.

The situation regarding the *ger toshav* may also have changed once Christianity began to become more popular. What was to differentiate the *ger toshav* from a Christian? Both would have forsaken idol worship. Both would keep the Noachide commandments. Perhaps this is the reason that the most stringent definition of a *ger toshav*, the last cited in our passage, was developed. That definition would differentiate the *ger toshav* from the Christian. According to that definition, a *ger toshav* would observe Shabbat and the Jewish holidays, the rite of circumcision and the laws of ritual purity. This *ger toshav* would be far more observant, Jewishly, than the Judeo-Christian.

This passage on the *ger toshav* ends with two contrasting stories which aptly show the ambivalence of the sages about these somewhat liminal individuals.

**GEMARA (64b):** Rav Yehudah sent a present (65a) to Avidarna on a heathen feastday (*eidam*), saying, "I know that he does not worship idols."

Rav Yosef said to him, "But it has been taught: Who is a *ger toshav*? Any [Gentile] who takes upon himself in the presence of three *chaveirim* not to worship idols!"—[Rav Judah replied], "This teaching only applies to the matter of supporting him."

[Rav Yosef] retorted, "But Rabbah bar Bar Hanah said in the name of R. Yohanan: A *ger toshav* who allows twelve months to pass without becoming circumcised is to be regarded as a heretic (*min*) among idolaters!" [Rav Judah answered], "This refers to the circumstance where he undertook to be circumcised but did not undergo the rite."

Rava once sent a present to Bar Shishakh on a heathen feastday (*eidam*), saying, "I know he does not worship idols." But he went [to visit Bar Shishakh and] found him sitting up to his neck in a bath of rosewater while naked harlots were standing before him. [Bar Shishakh] said to him, "Have you [Jews] anything like this in the World to Come?" He said to him, "We have much finer than this." He said, "Is there anything finer than this?" [Rava] said to him, "There is upon you the fear of the ruling power, but for us there will be no fear of the ruling power." He said to him, "What fear have I of the ruling power?" While they were sitting [together], the king's courier arrived and said to him [Bar Shishakh], "Arise, the king requires your presence." As he was about to depart [Bar Shishakh] said to [Rava], "May the eye burst that wishes to see evil of you!" To this Rava responded, "Amen," and his [Bar Shishakh's] eye burst.

The first case presented here concerns a non-Jew who is not circumcised but one to whom Rav Yehudah nonetheless sends a gift on a pagan holiday. Rav Yehudah apparently knows that this man does not worship idols, even though the man has never testified to this before three *chaveirim*. How, then, can Rav Yehudah justify sending him a gift on this day, a thing ordinarily forbidden (see Chapter One)? Rav Yehudah asserts that the person wanting the status of *ger toshav* has to testify before three *chaveirim* only if he wants to receive monetary support from the Jewish community. (A non-Jew who did not worship idols was to be supported from Jewish charitable funds.) This formal status was needed only for the sake of clarifying who was eligible for Jewish charity. It was not needed for normal social relations to be established. Rav Yosef then notes that this man is not circumcised and holds that a non-Jew who has become a *ger toshav* but who has not had himself circumcised within twelve months is to be considered a heretic. That is, such a person is not an idol-worshiper but he is no longer eligible for the status of *ger toshav*, having failed to observe one of the main commandments of Judaism. Rav Yehudah retorts that this is true only if the individual intended to be a *ger toshav* and took on this responsibility. However, this fellow Avidarna apparently does not want to be a *ger toshav*, neither in order to be supported by the Jewish community nor to be distinguished from a Judeo-Christian. He's simply a man who doesn't worship idols.

Here we have an example of a person who is in a state even less clear than that of a *ger toshav*. He's not an idolater, a *min*, a *ger toshav*, or a Jew. Rav Yosef wants to either include him or exclude him on the basis of the category *ger toshav*, and the criteria simply do not work in his situation. This story, which allows the ambiguity of Avidarna's status to stand, is followed by a more polemical tale that casts non-Jews who do not worship idols, but who are not *gerei toshav*, in a very negative light. These two stories reflect the ambiguity with which the sages considered these liminal individuals.

In the tale of Bar Shishakh, the notion of duplicitous power as the essence of idolatry is underscored. Bar Shishakh may not worship idols but he's far from a *ger toshav*. He doesn't understand the basis of Judaism: faithful relationships based on mutually binding responsibility. He does not practice it in his relationships with women, as is dramatically described, nor does he practice it or benefit from it in his relationship with earthly or heavenly authority. He cannot imagine anything greater than earthly pleasures. Dependent on earthly authorities, he cannot fathom the freedom that comes from entering into a mutual, exclusive relationship with God that demands moral behavior. He is brought low by the capriciousness of the earthly authorities who are as faithless as idolatrous gods.

He is also shown the power of God's faithfulness. Rava sees Bar Shishakh's true motivations and turns Bar Shishakh's hypocrisy on itself. Bar Shishakh is cursed with the very phrase he thought might gain him favor in Rava's eyes. This story demonstrates that merely forgoing the worship of idols themselves isn't enough to distance one's self from idolatry. Idolatry can infect human relationships, resulting in manipulative sex, blind devotion to political figures, and self-deception that becomes self-destruction. Thus, in the realm of intimate relationships, the realm of society, and the realm of the cosmos, this man is still attached to idolatry. Just because he doesn't worship idols doesn't blind the sages to his theology.

These two stories may be interpreted to suggest that the sages resisted involvement with non-Jews who did not take on the obligations of a *ger toshav*, even if these non-Jews gave up idolatry. A *ger toshav* is truly with the Jewish community, while this cannot be said of a non-Jew who does not worship idols. Today, the issue of the *ger toshav* has gained an added importance. Because of high rates of intermarriage, some communities would like to revive the institution of the *ger toshav* as a way of including non-Jews in Jewish life in some way. If this were to be attempted, according to our present reading of the texts, the *ger toshav* might have to adhere to the highest standard suggested to differentiate this person from a Christian. That is, this person might have to observe all the laws of Shabbat and the Festivals and would only be exempt from the obligation to eat kosher meat. Frankly, the Jewish community would have made a great step forward if we could raise all *Jews* to this level of observance.

Perhaps the more important practical wisdom of these passages is the recognition that there has always been a range of ways to be related to the Jewish community, both for Jews and for non-Jews, and that this range is still available. Then, too, the sages' continuous emphasis on one's inner state (e.g., Bar Shishakh's outer rejection of idols is deemed utterly empty because of his internal, continuing patterns of idolatry) provides the contemporary Jewish community with a meaningful set of criteria to measure any person's commitment to Jewish beliefs.

## How Wine Objectifies and Clarifies the Issue of Trust between Jews and Non-Jews

The Mishnah takes a very cautious stance when considering wine left in the presence of an idolater. It is simply not prudent to consider it undefiled by idolatry unless the idolater thought the Jew would soon return to reclaim his wine. When a Jew and an idolater eat together such a question arises.

> **MISHNAH (69a):** If he [a Jew] was eating with him [an idolater] at a table and he put a flask [of wine] on the table [and] a flask [of wine] on the side table, and he went out, that [wine] that is on the table is prohibited and that [wine] that is on the side table is permitted. And if he said to him [the idolater], "Mix [our wine] and drink," [the wine] that is on the side table is also forbidden. Open casks [of wine] are forbidden and sealed ones [are prohibited if the Jew were absent] for sufficient time [for the non-Jew] to open [a cask] and reseal [it] and let [the clay smeared over it] dry.

We note that the Mishnah posits a Jew and a non-Jew eating together harmoniously. Relations, then, between Jew and non-Jew in the Mishnah's idealistic vision are trusting enough that they can at least eat together. However, the issue of the wine shows that the trust is not complete; care must be taken lest the wine be contaminated by idolatry. This sidetable of which the Mishnah speaks was evidently a decorative buffet on which the food was laid out and so, perhaps, was not quite as near at hand when the host left, for example, to wash his hands. However, if the host said, "Help yourself to the bar!" then all the wine is considered susceptible to idolatrous contamination. This deep ambivalence, portrayed in the Mishnah's hypothetical situation, shows how the sages were engaged in that difficult, but necessary, exercise of drawing boundaries around a community in order to define it and safeguard its integrity.

The Gemara is engaged in this exercise, too. It, however, adds some nuances and offers us a glimpse of the way idolaters saw Jews:

> **GEMARA (70a):** A Jew and an idolater were sitting and drinking wine [together]. The Jew heard the sound of prayer in a synagogue; so he arose and went [there]. Rava said: The wine is permitted on the ground that [the idolater] must have thought, "He will remember the wine at any moment and return."
> 
> A Jew and an idolater were sitting in a ship. The Jew heard the

sound of the ram's horn announcing the advent of the Sabbath; so he left [the ship] and went ashore. Rava said: The wine is permitted on the ground that [the idolater] must have thought, "He will remember the wine at any moment and return." But if [it is supposed that the idolater would not think so] on account of its being the Sabbath, behold Rava has said, Issur the proselyte once told me, "When we were still Gentiles we declared that Jews do not observe the Sabbath, because if they did observe it how many purses would be found in the streets! I did not then know that we follow the view of Rabbi Yitshak who said: If a person is carrying a purse when the Sabbath begins he may carry it for distances of less than four cubits" (*B. Shabbat* 153b).

The first situation is straightforward. A Jew and an idolater are drinking wine together when the Jew gets up to go to synagogue. Rava holds that the Jew's wine, left sitting there with the idolater, is permitted because the idolater fears to touch it, thinking the Jew will return at any moment. This first story is confirmed by a second story. The Jew and the idolater are sitting on a boat this time, and the shofar blows announcing that Jews should stop working because Shabbat is approaching (see *Mishnah Sukkah* 5:5). The Jew leaves but the sages assume that the idolater will think the Jew will shortly return to claim his wine and, so, the wine would be untouched and therefore permitted. However, what if the idolater were knowledgeable about Judaism and knew that the Jew would not be returning? The retort to this argument comes from one who converted to Judaism. He said that idolaters didn't believe that Jews observed the Sabbath rules because people did not immediately throw down their money purses when Shabbat began. As an idolater, he was not aware of the ruling that allows a person to walk a few feet and then stop, walk another few feet and then stop, when they are carrying something when Shabbat happens to begin. Since idolaters thought that Jews simply didn't observe the Sabbath, the idolater drinking wine with the Jew on the boat would assume that the Jew would soon return and therefore the wine would be untainted by idolatry and safe to drink.

The sorts of "legal fictions" or, perhaps we might more accurately say "legal creativity," that allow Jews to balance their observance of Judaism with the needs of varied human experiences can appear hypocritical to an outsider (such as the solution for carrying a purse when Shabbat begins). The sages tried to maintain a balance in all the spheres of life: they did not utterly cut off the Jewish community from association with idolaters nor did they demand a Shabbat observance that would have been too onerous to bear. The price for this flexibility is a lack of one hundred percent consistency. And yet, how could it be otherwise? Judaism could either be flexible and live or be rigid and die. Thus, we will always have apparent inconsistencies and hypocrisies.

One last example of this phenomenon of leaving wine in the presence of a non-Jew is remarkable because it portrays a woman running a business:

GEMARA (70b): A [Jewish] woman who dealt in wine left the key of her door in charge of a pagan woman. Rabbi Yitshak said in the name of Rabbi Elazar: A similar occurrence was once brought before our House of Study [and they permitted the wine because] they said that she only entrusted her with watching the key. Abaye said: We have likewise learned similarly (*Mishnah Tohorot* 7:1): If a person entrusts his keys to an *am ha'arets*, his things that are in a state of ritual purity remain undefiled because he only entrusted him with watching the key.

One might compare this situation with leaving one's key with a neighbor today. You wouldn't assume that your neighbor would rub bacon fat into your counters while you were out of town for the weekend. Only the key was entrusted to the neighbor. She wasn't instructed to do anything inside the house and so she most likely did not do so. Similarly, the sages assume the idolatrous woman has not touched the wine. Again, notice how matter-of-factly it is assumed by the sages that a woman deals in wine, that she can cooperate with her non-Jewish neighbor, and that her actions have economic and ritual consequences that the sages take seriously. All of these are realities that, we might have thought, did not exist in the sages' days. Clearly, however, they did.

## The Grand Summation: Purity, Sex, Faithfulness, and the Jewish Faith in the World

Our tractate ends with a mishnah, and Gemara to it, that bring all our themes together. The mishnah here extends its examination of the infiltration of idolatry into Jewish life to its farthest reach. How does one expunge the idolatry that might have "seeped into" an idolater's cooking utensil?

> MISHNAH (75b): If [a Jew] purchases cooking utensils from an idolater, those which are customarily cleansed by immersion he must immerse, by scalding he must scald, by making white-hot in the fire he must make white-hot in the fire. A spit and grill must be made white-hot, but a knife may be polished and is then ritually clean.

One uses the customary methods of cleansing items to purify them from any idolatry. These goods must be purified before they are fit for Jewish use either by taking them to a *mikveh*, scalding them, heating them, or polishing them.

The Gemara ties this seemingly arcane teaching of the Mishnah to its closing image of the tractate, which is consistent with its constant theme: one's inner state, expressed in one's most private moments, is where the crucial tests of faith are passed or failed.

> GEMARA (76b): "But a knife may be polished and is then ritually clean." Rav Ukba bar Hama said: One plunges it ten times in soil [in addition to the polishing]. . . . Thus Mar Yehudah and Bati bar Tovi were sitting with King Shapur and a citron was set before them. [The king] cut a slice and ate it, and then cut a slice and handed it to Bati bar Tovi. After that he stuck [the knife] ten times in the ground, cut a slice [of the citron], and handed it to Mar Yehudah. Bati bar Tovi said to [the king], "Am I not a Jew!" He [the king] said to him, "Of him I am certain that he is observant [of Jewish law], but not of you." There are those who say he said to him, "Remember what you did [last] night!"

The knife is stabbed in the untilled ground ten times because the dirt acts as an abrasive agent, ridding the knife of any substance adhering to it. King Shapur (who apparently loved *etrogs*; his daughter smelled like one and she was her father's favorite perfume, B. *Ketubot* 61a) may be either Shapur I (reigned from 241–272 c.e.) or Shappur II (reigned from 309–379 c.e.) in Persia. King Shapur cuts some citron for Bati bar Tovi without putting the knife in the earth, while cleansing the knife for Mar Yehudah. Bati becomes insulted and the sages, through King Shapur, show that, while some appearances of hypocrisy are tolerable (such as the Sabbath rules about purses), true hypocrisy is not allowed. Apparently, King Shapur followed the Persian custom of sending each of the sages a slave girl to spend the night. Mar Yehudah sent his away while Bati allowed his to stay.

Thus, our tractate ends with a picture of maximum assimilation: the sages sit and eat with a king. These are not ordinary Jews, and this is not an ordinary non-Jew. This non-Jew, in contrast to those presented in Chapter One who tortured Jews, is respectful and knowledgeable about Jewish customs. He is even portrayed as understanding the deepest ideas of the sages: one's internal state is the most important. According to external criteria, both men should have had the knife cleaned for them in the ground. But their inner states were different, and King Shapur reflected that in his behavior. Faithfulness in relationships, and a shunning of promiscuity, are what Judaism is all about on the physical and spiritual levels.

This story hearkens back in many of its symbols to the Garden of Eden: we have here earth, holy fruit, a knife (like the sword that keeps Adam and Eve from returning to Eden, Genesis 3:24), sex, purity, faithfulness, and a king (here, Shapur; there, God). What allows one to stay with the king with honor? Faithfulness in relationships and approaching the system that is Judaism with integrity. This is what allows us to remain in the Garden of Eden.

# Halakhah

In the first two volumes of *The Talmud for Beginners*, the halakhic outcomes of Talmudic passages were presented in appendices. Because Rabbi Steinsaltz has not yet translated this volume, his précis of the *halakhah* is currently unavailable. In addition, many of the topics raised in this tractate are currently under vigorous discussion in the Jewish world. Any attempt to summarize the *halakhah* would fail, since different movements of Judaism have such widely disparate views on these matters. Readers with halakhic questions are urged to consult their own rabbis and teachers.

# Glossary

**Aliyah/Aliyot:** Literally, "going up." The act of saying the blessings over the Torah reading during worship services and/or actually reading from the Torah. This word may also refer to the person who has a synagogue honor. In addition, other honors during the service (e.g., opening the ark) are called *aliyot*. In contemporary usage it may also mean immigrating to Israel.

**Am Ha'arets/Amei ha'arets:** Literally, "a people of the land." An idiom designating a Jewishly unlearned person and/or a person who behaves boorishly. In the sages' days, it was a person who was not scrupulous in observing the commandments, particularly those regarding ritual purity and agricultural taxes.

**Amidah/Amidot/Tefillah/Tefillot/Shemonah Esrei:** Literally, "standing," "the prayer" and "eighteen." The prayer par excellance in Judaism. It contains nineteen benedictions and is said standing three times each day.

**Amora/Amoraim:** The sages who expounded the Mishnah, thereby composing the Gemara. The Gemara and Mishnah together form the Talmud. The period of the *Amoraim* extends from the end of the third to the end of the fifth century. Amoraim lived in both Palestine and Babylonia.

**Aramaic:** One of the languages used in the Talmud. It is similar in some ways to Hebrew. It developed after Hebrew and was the language of the general population in the days of the *Amoraim*.

**Aleinu:** Literally, "it is on us" or "it is incumbent upon us [to praise God]." A prayer near the end of most Jewish worship services during which worshipers bow toward the ark, which holds the Torah.

**Azarah:** "Courtyard" in the Temple. There were courtyards for women, lay Israelites, and priests outside the Temple building itself, which held the ark in the Holy of Holies.

**Ba'al Teshuvah/Ba'alei Teshuvah:** Literally, "a master of return." A Jew who has taken on a more observant lifestyle.

**Babylonia:** In Hebrew, *Bavel*. During the sages' era, Babylonia was centered in the area between the Tigris and Euphrates Rivers (modern day Iraq).

**B.C.E.** Before the Common Era; B.C.

**Baraita/Baraitot:** Literally, "external." A source from the *Tannaitic* era that was not included in the Mishnah of R. Judah HaNasi but is cited by the *Amoraim*.

**Bat Kol:** Literally, "a voice from Heaven." There are four possible meanings for this concept: 1. Popular opinion. 2. Listening to children, especially asking them what verse they are reading and taking it as prophecy. 3. An echo: *bat kol* can be taken literally as "the daughter of a sound." 4. *Bat Kol Min HaShamayim*: A voice from heaven. This is true revelation, however, it cannot be used as a basis for adjudicating Jewish law.

**Bimah:** Literally, "a stage or platform." The raised dais from which Torah is read in the synagogue.

**Birkat HaMazon:** The blessing over food said after a meal. It is derived from Deuteronomy 8:10, "When you have eaten and are satisfied, you will bless the Lord your God for the good land He has given you."

**Chag/Chagim:** Literally, "festival." The festivals ordained in the Torah—Passover, Sukkot, and Shavuot—as well as Rosh HaShanah and Yom Kippur, share many of the same restrictions that apply to Shabbat, such as the prohibitions against carrying items from one domain to another.

**Chakham:** Literally, "a wise man." A sage.

**Chol:** Secular, profane, not holy.

**C.E.** The Common Era, i.e., A.D.

**Chaveir:** "An associate or colleague." The opposite of an *Am Ha'arets*. Someone who was dedicated to the strict observance of the mitzvot.

**Cohen/Cohanim:** Priests who could officiate in the Temple.

**Cohen Gadol:** The High Priest. This priest was the only one who could perform the Yom Kippur service. He had special clothes, perquisites, and a unique, high status.

**Drash:** The act of making an exposition of a biblical text.

**Drashah/Drashot:** An exposition of a biblical text.

**Frum:** Religious; religiously observant.

**Gemara:** The commentary on the Mishnah, composed by the *Amoraim*. It contains *baraitot*, *aggadot*, and *Amoraic* discussions. The Babylonian Gemara was formulated between 200–500 C.E.

**Ger Toshav:** A resident alien in the Land of Israel. A non-Jew who does not worship idols and who may observe other rules of Jewish life.

**Halakhah:** "The Way." Jewish law.

**Havdalah:** "Difference." The ceremony that concludes the Sabbath on Saturday evening. Prayers are said over wine, spices, and a braided candle.

**Hefker:** Ownerless property. The owner has completely relinquished all claims to his property to make it *hefker*.

**Heichal:** The sanctuary. The inner section of the Temple that contained the menorah (candelabrum), gold table, and incense altar.

**High Priest:** See Cohen Gadol.

**Kashrut:** The rules outlining permissible and forbidden foods in Judaism.

**Ketubah/Ketubot:** A Jewish wedding contract.

**Kiddush HaShem:** "The Sanctification of the Name." Martyrdom.

**Kiddush (Kedushat HaYom):** "The Holiness of the Day." The prayer said to sanctify Shabbat and festivals. Said during the *Amidah* and over wine on Friday evenings, that is, on Shabbat.

**Kodesh:** "Holy." Opposite of *chol*.

**Kiddushin:** "Betrothal." A woman becomes betrothed to a man with money (usually a ring) or a document. Today it is performed at the same time as a wedding.

**Lashon Harah:** Literally, "bad speech." A complex system of laws against gossiping, even if what is said is true.

**Levi/L'vi'im:** A descendant of the tribe of Levi. These men functioned as singers and musicians in the Temple.

**Lulav:** Literally, "a palm branch." This term almost always refers to the four species (palm, myrtle, willow, and citron) waved together on the holiday of Sukkot.

**Mezuzah:** "Doorpost." A parchment on which are written the words of Deuteronomy 6:4–9 and Deuteronomy 11:13–21. The parchment is then affixed to the doorpost of a dwelling.

**Midrash/Midrashim:** Expositions of biblical texts in rabbinic literature.

**Mikveh:** A Jewish ritual bath used for purification and conversion to Judaism.

**Min/Minim:** "Kind, species." A heretic, especially members of early Jewish Christian sects or Gnostics.

**Minor:** (Hebrew, *katan*) A person who has not reached maturity, generally accepted as up to the age of 12 for girls and 13 for boys.

**Mishnah/Mishnayot:** "Teaching." Refers to the collection of *Tannaitic* learning compiled by Rabbi Judah HaNasi in 200 C.E. and to individual segments within that compilation.

**Mitzvah:** "Commandment." A deed that one must perform or an action one must refrain from doing that is derived from the Torah or from a dictate of the rabbis.

**Mumar:** An apostate Jew.

**Nechemtah/Nechemtot:** A message of comfort and hope that concludes prayers and sections of Talmud. These often make mention of the Exodus from Egypt, the paradigm of redemption.

**N'veilah:** An animal's carcass. An animal that died of natural causes rather than being slaughtered in the way mandated by *kashrut*.

**Oral Torah:** In Hebrew, *Torah sheb'al peh*. The complement to the Written Torah, composed by the sages.

**Our Rabbis Taught:** In Hebrew, *Tanu Rabbanan*. A technical phrase that introduces a *baraita*.

**Oveid Kochavim:** Literally, "a star-worshiper." That is, an idolater.

**Pesach:** "To pass over." The Festival in the spring that celebrates the exodus from Egypt. This holiday marks the end of winter.

**Proselyte:** A person who converts to Judaism. In Hebrew, a *ger* (male) or *gioret* (female).

**Seah:** A liquid measure of about 2 gallons (about 8 liters). It can also be used as a measure of solids.

**Seder:** Literally, "order." The service held to commemorate the holiday of Pesach.

**Scriptures:** The Torah, Prophets, and Writings. Torah is considered to be divinely revealed in traditional Judaism. Prophets and Writings have a lower level of holiness and authority than the Torah.

**Shabbat:** The seventh day of the week. A day of rest that lasts from Friday sundown to Saturday sundown.

**Shema:** "Hear." The central creed of Judaism. Consists of Deuteronomy 6:4–9, Deuteronomy 11:13–21, and Numbers 15:37–41. The first line must be said with intention.

**Shofar:** A ram's horn (or other animal horn such as antelope) used as a musical instrument.

**Sotah:** A woman suspected of adultery by her husband, warned by her husband before witnesses to stay away from a specific man, and observed alone with that man. She must undergo the rite of the bitter waters to clear her name as outlined in Numbers 5:11–31.

**Stamma/Stammaim:** "The Silent Ones" or perhaps better, "the Anonymous Ones." The sages of the period after the close of the Talmud (after 500).

**Sukkah:** Literally, "booth." The temporary structure Jews live and eat in for the harvest festival, Sukkot.

**S'vara:** Literally, "reason." A logical idea that has no scriptural or rabbinic source. The arguments that support such reasonable ideas.

**Tallit:** The garment that has the *tsitsit* tied to its four corners. A Jewish garment worn during prayer. (When the *tsitsit* are worn all day long, under one's clothes, they are attached to a garment called *arbah kanfot*, "the four corners.")

**Tanach:** The Hebrew acronym for the Scriptures. Torah, *Neviim* (Prophets), and *Ketuvim* (Writings).

**Tanna/Tannaim:** A teacher of the Oral Law. The *Tannaim* are the sages of the Mishnaic period, 70–220 C.E.

**Tefillah/Tefillin:** "Phylacteries." Cube-shaped leather boxes that are tied to the hand and head. They contain the following passages written on parchment: Deuteronomy 6:4–9, Deuteronomy 11:13–21, Exodus 13:1–10, and Exodus 13:11–16.

**Tekhelet:** Blue dye. The special blue dye used on the fringes (*tsitsit*) of one's garment (see Numbers 15:38). The dye was made from the murex snail and was extremely expensive.

**Tisha B'Av:** Literally, "the Ninth of Av." This is the Jewish day of mourning for the destruction of both the first and second Temples held on the ninth of the Jewish month of Av. The Book of Lamentations is read on this day.

**Torah:** The first five books of the Bible: Genesis, Exodus, Leviticus, Numbers, and Deuteronomy. Also used for Jewish learning in general. This book in scroll form is called a Sefer Torah.

**Toraitic:** From, or derived from, the first five books of the *Tanach*.

**Tosefta/Toseftot:** Literally, "addition" or "supplement." *Tannaitic* material collected into a compendium as an addition to the Mishnah. *Toseftot* do not have the authoritative stature of *mishnayot*.

**Tractate:** A volume of Talmud.

**Tsitsit:** The fringes on a *tallit*, a ritual prayer shawl, or on a four-cornered piece of cloth worn under the clothes as a fulfillment of the commandment in Numbers 15:37–41, which orders Jews to wear these fringes on the corners of their garments.

**Ulam:** The entrance hall of the Sanctuary building in the Temple.

**Yei'ush:** The act of an owner's despairing of ever recovering a lost or stolen piece of property. This makes the article ownerless, *hefker*.

**Yom Kippur:** The Day of Atonement on the tenth of *Tishrei* (in the fall).

**Writings:** In Hebrew, *Ketuvim*. The third section of the *Tanach*, which contains the Psalms, Proverbs, Job, the Five Scrolls, Daniel, Ezra-Nehemia, and Chronicles.

**Yerushalmi:** The Talmud composed in the Land of Israel. It differs in many ways from the Babylonian Talmud and is not as widely studied. It was completed in approximately 400 C.E.

**Zimmun:** The invitation to say grace that precedes *Birkat HaMazon.*

# Bibliography

Albek, H. (1959). *Mishnah* (Six Volumes). Tel Aviv: D'vir.
An excellent, modern commentary on the Mishnah. In Hebrew.

Aries, P., and Georges, D. (1987). *A History of Private Life from Pagan Rome to Byzantium*. Cambridge: Belknap/Harvard.
A readable, lavishly illustrated volume.

Council of Jewish Federations (CJF) (1991). *Highlights of the CJF 1990 National Jewish Population Survey*. New York: CJF.
A thorough statistical study of the American Jewish community.

Elazar, D. J. (1976). *Community and Polity*. Philadelphia: JPS.
A classic treatment of American Jewish society.

Gitin, S. (1990). Ekron of the Philistines, Part II: Olive-Oil Suppliers of the World. *BAR*, 16/2, pp. 33–42, 59.

Goodblatt, D. M. (1975). *Rabbinic Instruction in Sasanian Babylonia*. Leiden: E. J. Brill.
A scholarly analysis of how the sages learned and taught.

Goodenough, E. (1956). *Jewish Symbols in the Greco–Roman Period*, vol. 6. New York: Pantheon.
This thirteen-volume work, with numerous illustrations, is one of the best historical considerations of the rabbinic era.

Halbertal, M., and Avishai, M. (1992). *Idolatry*, trans. N. Goldblum. Cambridge: Harvard University Press.
A thoughtful examination of the topic of idolatry.

Hammer, R. (1986). *Sifre: A Tannaitic Commentary on the Book of Deuteronomy*. New Haven: Yale University Press.
An excellent translation of this midrashic work, with copious notes.

147

Herford, R. T. (1903). *Christianity in Talmud and Midrash*. Hoboken, NJ: KTAV.
A classic consideration of the role of Christians and *minim* in rabbinic literature.

Jacobsen, T. (1976). *The Treasures of Darkness: A History of Mesopotamian Religion*. New Haven: Yale University Press.
A classic, scholarly study of idolatrous worship in Mesopotamia.

Katz, J. (1961). *Exclusiveness and Tolerance*. New York: Behrman House.
This book traces the development of the Jewish community's relationship to the world around it through the medieval era.

Kuhn, T. S. (1970). *The Structure of Scientific Revolutions*, 2nd ed., enlarged. Chicago: University of Chicago Press.
An important theoretical work that describes how intellectual progress is made.

Lauterbach, J. Z. (1961). *Mekhilta*, 3 vols. Philadelphia: JPS.
A translation of the early midrash of the book of Exodus.

Neusner, J., trans. (1986). *The Talmud on the Land of Israel*, vol. 20, *Hagigah and Moed Qatan*, pp. 45–50. Chicago: University of Chicago Press.

Oppenheimer, A. (1977). *The 'Am Ha-aretz*. Leiden: E. J. Brill.
A scholarly examination of the topic of *amei ha'arets*.

Sarna, N. M. (1966). *Understanding Genesis: The Heritage of Biblical Israel*. New York: Schocken.
A scholarly but readable commentary on the book of Genesis.

Steinsaltz, A. (1989). *The Talmud: The Steinsaltz Edition, A Reference Guide*. New York: Random House.
Rabbi Steinsaltz's encyclopedic guide to the sages' era, geography, terminology, and theology.

Tham, H. (1994). *Men and Other Strange Myths: Poems and Art*. Colorado Springs: Three Continents Press.
Poems by a Chinese-Jewish writer.

# For Further Reading

Those seeking some basic resources on Judaism might want to look at the following:

## Torah Commentaries

The Hertz Pentateuch (Soncino Press), Plaut Torah (U.A.H.C.) and Stone Torah (Artscroll) editions are all good, one-volume commentaries. The Jewish Publication Society commentary, in five volumes, is truly excellent, although somewhat expensive.

## Computer Resources

Many resources are available on CD-ROM in English, such as the Soncino Talmud, Midrash Rabbah and Zohar (a Jewish mystical work).

## Reference Works

The Encyclopedia Judaica is the standard Jewish reference work and comes in a "Junior Judaica" version for children.

## Talmud

*The Talmud: The Steinsaltz Edition,* published by Random House, now includes the tractates of Baba Metsia, Taanit, Ketubot and Sanhedrin as well as the Reference Guide. The Soncino translation is complete and available in book and CD-ROM forms.

# Index of Sources Cited

## Psalms

1:1–6, Ch. 1
34:13–15, Ch. 1
49:6, Ch. 1
104:26, Ch. 1
109:22, Ch. 1
121:8, Ch. 1

## Proverbs

9:12, Ch. 1
13:11, Ch. 1

## Ecclesiastes

7:8, Ch. 3
10:8, Ch. 2

## Mishnah

*Peah* 1:1, Ch. 1
*Sukkah* 5:5, Ch. 5
*Taanit* 4:6, Ch. 1
*Kiddushin* 4:1,
   Ch. 2
*Sanhedrin*, 7:6,
   Ch. 4
*Pirkei Avot* 1:1,
   Introduction
*Tohorot* 7:1, Ch. 5

## Tosefta

*Avodah Zarah*
   7:16, Ch. 5
*Avodah Zarah*
   8:4, Ch. 1
*Avodah Zarah*
   8:4–6, Ch. 5

*Hullin* 2:22–23,
   Ch. 2
2:22–23, Ch. 2

## Yerushalmi

*Hagigah* 2:1, 77b,
   Ch. 1, Ch. 3

## Bavli

## Berachot

6a, Introduction
48a, Ch. 4
61b, Ch. 1

## Shabbat

54b, Ch. 1
127a, Ch. 1
153b, Ch. 5

## Eruvin

54b, Ch. 1

## Pesachim

25a–b, Ch. 2
49a, Ch. 4
66a, Ch. 1
66b, Ch. 1
34b, Ch. 1
61b, Ch. 1
108b, Ch. 4

## Yoma

85b, Ch. 2

## Taanit

7a–b, Ch. 1

## Megillah

25b, Ch. 4
26a, Ch. 4
26b, Ch. 4

## Yebamot

122a, Ch. 4

## Ketubot

61a, Ch. 5

## Kiddushin

30b, Ch. 1

## Baba Kamma

38a, Ch. 1
82a, Ch. 1

## Baba Metsia

59a, Ch. 2
61b, Ch. 2
62a, Ch. 1

## Baba Batra

17a, Ch. 1
164b, Ch. 4

## Sanhedrin

7b, Ch. 4
56a–b, Ch. 5
74a, Ch. 2

# Index

## ABOUT THE AUTHOR

Judith Z. Abrams is a woman with a mission: She wants to bring the beauty of Talmud to as many people, and with as much depth, as possible. To that end, she has published many books on the Talmud, including *The Talmud for Beginners, Volumes I and II* and, with her husband, Steven, *Jewish Parenting: Rabbinic Insights, Learn Talmud: How to Use the Talmud: The Steinsaltz Edition*, and *The Women of the Talmud* (all Jason Aronson Inc). She earned her Ph.D. in Rabbinic literature from the Baltimore Hebrew University and teaches across the country. She is the founder and director of Maqom: A School for Adult Talmud Study, where anyone can learn, regardless of their background. Maqom classes are also available on the internet (http://www.compassnet. com/~maqom/and at http://www.jcn18.com/forum/study/). She lives in Houston with her husband, Steven, and their three children, Michael, Ruth, and Hannah.